Environmental
Design
Best Selection 2

Landscape design City planning, Townscapes, Road plans, Park plans, Plazas, Landscaping, Exterior plans, etc. Residential Environmental design Houses, Duplexes, Vacation homes and related exterior design projects.
Public & Office Environmental design Welfare and social facilities, Clinics, Motor vehicle departments, Municipal offices, Banks, Schools, Museums, Business

buildings and related outdoor design and landscaping. Commercial and Leisure Environmental design Stores, Commercial complexes, Shopping Malls, Acades, Hotels, Sports facilities, Recreational facilities and other related outdoor design.

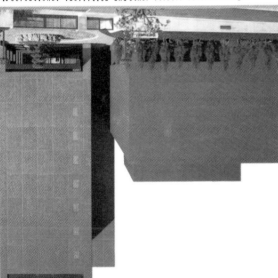

環境デザインベストセレクション②

より良い環境デザインに向けて

「環境は人をつくる」とはよくいわれることである。人づくりには教育の力が大きくはたらくことは確かだが，環境が人々に与える影響力は，もっともっと大きくて，はかり知れないものがあるといえよう。

人は毎日の暮らしのなかで，見て，考え，学び，工夫しながら体や心をはぐくんでいく。

環境には自然が与えてくれた世界と，人間が目的をもって創っていった世界とがあるが，「人をつくる」要素はどちらにも同等に，含まれている。「人をつくる」のにふさわしい環境は，いろいろな要素の複合化によって可能になる。人をつくる環境は，人間が環境をどのようにコントロールし，デザインしたかによって質的に向上したり，低下したりする。

都市をめぐる環境のデザインは，そうした意味で，現代生活者にとって重要な生活テーマになりはじめている。

都市生活者にとって，現代の都市環境は必ずしも快適とはいえず，むしろ「人をつくる」に，ふさわしくない傾向にあったのは事実である。そうした反省から近年，日本の大都市をはじめとする“環境づくり”はめざましく向上した。それは都市生活者の経済的な余裕にうらづけされた，精神の開放ともいえる。日本人は，見る，聴く，触れるなどの五感と，遊び心を満たす環境デザインを求めはじめている。

国連は，1987年を「国際居住年」と定め，より良い居住環境，住まい方の見直しを世界に問うている。わが国でも，政府をはじめ民間デベロッパーなどが，その主旨にもとづいていて諸々のイベントを開催し，環境デザインへの関心も高まりをたすけている。
「複合都市，情報都市，24時間都市」といったキーワードに示されるように，都市は国際的な情報ネットワークのもとにはじめて機能することになり，ひとり東京やニューヨーク，パリ，ロンドンが独立しては都市としての機能をはたし得なくなったことの実証でもあ

った。そうした意味で，都市環境のデザインを思考するには，国際的同時性のなかで機能するデザインコンセプトを強く認識しなければならない。

1986年3月，東京の赤坂と六本木にまたがって大規模再開発事業が実現した。アークヒルズである。超高層オフィスビル，住宅棟，都市型ホテル，テレビスタジオ，コンサートホールなどを組み合わせた複合都市である。オフィス棟は，テレビ会議システム，高速デジタル回線網などの最先端の情報・通信技術を利用できるようになっている。住宅棟は高級ホテル並みの生活関連サービスを提供している。まさに国際化に対応した，設備やサービスをそろえたのが大きな特徴である。20年近い歳月をかけた土地の権利調整，街づくりの手法は，今後の大規模な都市開発事業の有効なサンプルとして位置づけておきたい。

こうした大規模な開発による環境デザインにかぎらず，住空間デザイン，公共デザイン，商業空間デザイン，レジャー空間デザイン，さらにはサインデザイン，ストリートファニチュアーデザインなどの向上は，年々見るべきものがあり，総合的なデザイン効果が，現代の生活環境に活力を与えている。

こうした環境デザインの総合的な実態を，この本から感じとることができるであろう。日本の，自然と歴史，文明と文化の積み重ねとしての環境デザインの成果がここに集められている。これらの実績は，未来の日本の環境デザインにとって大きなプラス要素として機能しつづけるであろう。

集録された245点の作品は，多数の図版・写真により構成している。自由な意志により，自由に集結したこれらの作品は，それぞれの個性を発揮し，輝いてみえる。それは明日へのより良い環境デザインに向けて可能性を暗示しているのである。

「環境デザイン・ベストセレクション」編集委員会

Tward a better environment

It is often said that 'man is a product of his environment'. Of course the influence of education on human development is also considerable. but the effect of environment is even greater, and in many ways unknowable.

Physical and spiritual growth is achieved naturally, in everyday life, through work, study, thought and perceptions, and both the natural and man-made worlds provide stimulus in this process of creating a human being. Through a synthesis of the right elements from each world (natural and man-made) the human being is created. But the quality of the environment, upon which human development depends, is determined by the effort and design man puts into creating it.

In urban environmental design this is becoming an increasingly important theme.

Modern life in the urban environment is not, unfortunately, the best of all possible. In fact there is a tendency to argue it is unsuitable to its purpose of 'human creation'.

The recent environmental design trends in Japan are a reflection of this and an awakening to the idea of 'environment-building'. It might also be said that they follow on recent economic affluence and heightened appreciation for man's spiritual life. Japanese are now demanding that their environment satisfy the five senses and provide for their spiritual pleasure as well.

The United Nations designated 1986 'The year of the Home'; a year to work for a better living environment. Our government as well has supported the theme of public development and sponsored various events which have helped to increase appreciation of environmental design.

Ideas such as the integrated city, the 'smart city', or the 24-hour city, reflect the internationalization of the city and its newfound potential within the worldwide communication network. New York, Tokyo, London and Paris, are no longer isolated island cities, and this fact is changing the philosophy of urban design. In 1986 a major construction project was completed in Tokyo's Roppongi and Akasaka districts. Ark Hills is a 'smart city', a self-contained city including high-rise office buildings, apartments, a luxury hotel, TV studio and concert hall. The offices have access to televised meeting systems and a state of the art, digital, fully integrated communication network, while the apartment complex offers services on par with the finest hotels. Meeting the call to internationalize was Ark Hills aim, and its services and technological innovations reflect this. Twenty years of city planning and reclamation work should serve as a model for future large scale urban development projects.

But attention is not limited to the 'smart city' developments alone. The improvement of housing and community design, commercial and leisure areas, parks, street furniture and sign design is just as essential. These environmental elements, integrally designed, all contribute to the quality and efficiency of modern life.

This book offers a look at actual integrated environmental design in Japan. The interaction of nature and history, culture and thought, is present throughout these works. The inspiration for future environmental design is to be found here.

245 of works presented here, including many photographs, illustrations and renderings, were selected liberally and thus display considerable individuality. Their radiance is bright, illuminating the way toward the better environmental design of the future.

Editorial Committee for "Selection of Best Environmental Designs"

目　次

CONTENTS

● 凡例

a. 作品名

b. 所在地

c. クライアント

d. ディレクター, etc.

e. イラストレーター, エージェンシー, エンジニア, 音楽, 監理者, 企画構成, キャラクター, グラフィックデザイナー, コーディネーター, 照明, 設計, 設計監修, 設計協力, 造形デザイナー, 彫刻, テクニカルデザイナー, 展示設計, デザイナー, デザイン計画, 人形デザイン, 背景画, プランナー, プロジェクトマネージャー, プロダクトマネージャー, プロモーター, マネージャー, モニュメント, etc.

f. 施工者

g. 撮影者

h. コメント

i. 主な使用材料

j. 応募代表者

● Caption Information

a. Project name

b. Location

c. Client

d. Director, etc.

e. Illustrators, Agencies, Engineering, Musical Scores, Management, Drafting, Planning, Graphic Design, Lighting, Model Design, Technical Design, Sculpting, Exhibition Planning, Promotion, etc.

f. Coordinating

g. Photographer

h. Comments

i. Materials

j. Representatives/Contributors

ENVIRONMENTAL DESIGN BEST SELECTION 2

Copyright © 1987
by Graphic-sha Publishing Co., Ltd.
ISBN4-7661-0444-7
Manufactured in Japan
First Edition October 1987
Graphic-sha Publishing Co., Ltd.
1-9-12 Kudankita Chiyoda-ku
Tokyo 102 Japan

都会のなかの未来都市への試み
アークヒルズ誕生

An Attempt at Creating A Futuristic City within the City
The Birth of Ark Hills

20

24時間稼働するインテリジェント・オフィスビル，国際派ビジネスマンが利用するインテリジェント・ホテル，ニュース番組専用のTVスタジオ，クラシック音楽専用のコンサートホール，高級ホテル並みの生活関連サービスを提供する都市型マンション，緑と水に満ちたプラザ，コミュニティ施設群……。

これらがみごとに融合し，調和して，5.6㌶という広さを感じさせないほど多彩な内容をもつ「アークヒルズ」。1986年3月に完成。ところは東京の赤坂・六本木・虎ノ門をむすぶ三角の中心地である。この一帯は日本の政治・経済・文化の中心をなす，いわば東京の顔といってよい地区である。同時に，世界のあらゆる情報が集まり，発信される機能を備えなければならない。そうしたビジネスとして必要な機能を満しながら，人間の生活と文化機能をどのように複合することができるか，いわば世界が期待するなかでの開発であった。

アークヒルズ（ARK HILLS）の環境デザインの特色は，文字が示すとおり「丘の段差」を利用した点にある。その高低差は約18m（建物にして6階分）である。

この丘陵地は，もとは数百戸の木造家屋が密集し，消防車や救急車も容易に入れないほどの狭い道でつながれていた。そこに住む人たちの要望やニーズを満足させながら，しかも東京の都心としての公共性の高い機能を同時に満たすという両面を解決するという開発であった。丘陵の高低差を有効に生かした環境デザインは，多様な機能を段階的に包みこんで解決している。

最も低く六本木通りに面したゾーンには，オフィスとホテルを配しその効率的利用が考慮されている。中段には商業施設，プラザ，ホール，TVスタジオなどがあり，最も高いエリアには住まいを配し，その周辺は小鳥の集まる庭園，緑地で囲む構成となっている。特にコンサートホールやTV

スタジオの屋上に設けられた段々の散策路は，こうした傾斜地の条件から生まれてきたものである。

個々の環境デザインをみると細かいところまで配慮と演出がある。そのいくつかを挙げると……。

庭園の最上段にバードウォッチング施設と小鳥が集まる実のなる造園。アークプラザにある可動パーゴラや高層の圧迫感をやわらげるコリドール。広場を受けとめるように位置している滝は，舞台のカーテンが閉じたり開いたりするように水の表情が変化する演出。コンサートホール入口の上部にあって時間がくると壁面が開いて演奏がはじまるパイプオルガン。複雑な機能を表示するサイン群。都バス乗り場のシェルター。オフィスビルの導入部が，外部の床と内部の床が一体になっていて，抵抗感を少しでもへらす配慮……。

21世紀にむけての未来型環境デザインもある。その意味で次のふたつは見落すことはできない。

そのひとつは，太陽光を集光する"ひまわり"

1　太陽光を集光する「ひまわり」
The Himawari sunlight collector

2　「ひまわり」から集光した太陽光を拡散して植物を育てる
「太陽光植物ドーム」
Light from the Himawari diffused over greenery in the 'plant dome.'

3　オフィス・ビルの入り口にある竹林にも「ひまわり」からの
光が降り注ぐ
Sunlight from the Himawari bathes a grove of bamboo at the entrance
to the office building

からファイバーで地下やロビーに運び，ランプで拡散し植物を育てるシステム。

もうひとつは，「呼吸する空調」。超高層ビルでは各部屋ごとに空気を吸い込むことは不可能だが，外壁の縦格子のポケットにユニットの空調機をはめ込むと，呼吸が可能になる。赤坂ツインタワーではじめて試みられて，アークヒルズで本格的に採用されたという。

こうした環境デザインのひとつひとつは，アークヒルズの開発コンセプトにもとづいて展開され

ている。開発主体と住民とが20年の歳月をかけてつくりあげた，街づくりの共通意識があってこそ，アークヒルズは可能になった。土地の権利調整から街づくりデザインまでのプロセスは，これから生れる大規模な都市開発により影響を与えるにちがいない。

先端技術による情報の街のデザインが，土地を分断しての“点としてのビル開発”ではなく“面としての大きな街区再開発”として達成できたことが意義深い。新しい都市づくり，街づくりのお

手本となり，生き生きとした運営によって，世界からの人，物，情報が交流しあえる，東京の格調ある名所として親しまれ，新しい都市文明の芽生えることを期待したい。

同時にアークヒルズの環境デザインの志向は，未来にむけていくつもの示唆と方向性を示し，その環境力は計り知れないものがある。

4

5

7

4 ビジネス空間にも憩いの木々を植樹
Trees and plants thriving in the business center

5 ビジネス空間にも憩いの木々を植樹
Trees and plants thriving in the business center

6 人の多く集まるホテルのロビーこそ緑が必要
Greenery is needed where people congregate, as in the hotel lobby

7 大都会に生活する人々の憩いの場
A relaxation area within the metropolis

A twenty-four hour "intelligent" office building and hotel for international businessmen ; a TV studio devoted exclusively to news and information ; a classical music concert hall ; urbantype apartments with the daily life services as good as those of a luxury hotel ; a central plaza with flowing water and abundant greenery ; and community establishments.

"Ark Hills" -that is provided with these diversified functions which have been so handsomely blended in harmony with each other

that it defies all attempts to conjecture its area, which actually is as expansive as 5.6 hectares. This was completed in March of 1986, and built in the center of a triangle formed by the connections of three points, i.e., Roppongi, Akasaka, and Toranomon-the district of, say, the face of Tokyo-the economic, political, and cultural center of Japan. Ark Hills, therefore, is required be possessed of business functions such as collecting every worldwide information on the one hand and

dispatching information to the world on the other. While meeting the requirements of such functions, the scheme had to solve the problem of how to successfully reconcile human living with cultural functions. Thus, the development was conducted with the worldwide expectations focused on this very point.

The features of the environmental design of Ark Hills, as the name suggests, lies in taking full advantage of its topology. Ark Hills is located on hills with the difference in level

8

9

10

11

8　昼のひととき，公園はビジネス・マンでにぎわう
Businessmen fill the park at lunchtime

9　パーゴラは超高層ビルからの圧迫感をなくす効果がある
The pergola relieves the sense of pressure from high-rise buildings

10　パーゴラは超高層ビルからの圧迫感をなくす効果がある
The pergola relieves the sense of pressure from high-rise buildings

11　イベント・スペース
The event space

reaching a full eighteen meters, the equivalent of six stories.

Originally the hillock was an area where hundreds of wooden houses were densely built-up, accessed by roads so narrow that neither fire trucks nor ambulances could maneuver easily. The development of the area involved the dual task of meeting the local residents needs and at the same time giving the city an excellent civic facility.

The environmental design which effectively utilized the differences in hill level has been successfully achieved by arranging a variety of functions in stages.

The placement of the office buildings and hotel along Roppongi Boulevard, at the lowest elevation, was a considered strategy for the effective use of such services. At the middle level the plaza, commercial area, TV studio and concert hall were constructed. On the highest ground, in an area interspersed with gardens and green zones where a flock of birds

hovers around, living accommodations were established. The walkways laid above the concert hall and TV studio are good examples of the efforts to wisely utilize the contoured landscape.

Looking deep into the individual environmental design reveals every contrivance and nice presentation that have been effected in detail. Some examples are summarized as follows : There are bird watching equipment and a landscape at the highest level where birds

12 パーゴラは超高層ビルからの圧迫感をなくす効果がある
The pergola relieves the sense of pressure from high-rise buildings

13 パブリック・スペース
Public Space

14 全環境都市「アークヒルズ」を案内するサイン
A guide ro Ark Hills, the omni-environment city

15 ビルの中を通ってる公道
An interior public walkway

gather and plants bear fruit. At the Ark Plaza, there are a movable pergola and corridors diminishing the dominating effect of the high-rise structures. A waterfall located in a position to receive the Plaza presents changing expressions like the appearance of a moving stage curtain, enhancing the atmosphere of the central plaza. Above the entrance to the concert hall, there is a pipe organ which starts playing music to announce the time with the automated facade open. Signboards with complex functions, bus stops with comfortable shelters, floors that run from inside to without cleavage, reducing the sense of opposition…

There are important considerations in the modern environmental designs for the 21st Century. Two design innovations which cannot be overlooked, in this sense, include the gathering and transferring of sunlight from the "Himawari" system via glass fiber conductors to the basement or lobbies in the building and dispersing the light with lamps, so that plants can flourish. The second is "breathing air conditioning system". Making fresh air available to every room in a high-rise structure is impoassible, but installing air conditioners in the pocket of the vertical lattice in the outer walls improves circulation. This system was first implemented on a partial basis at Akasaka Towers, and fully as a basic system at Ark Hills.

These distinct elements of environmental design were all developed based on the design

16

17

18

19

16　全環境都市「アークヒルズ」を案内するサイン
A guide ro Ark Hills, the omni-environment city

17　地下6階を埋め尽くすTV局放送センター
Broadcasting center of the TV station, which has six lower floors

18　超高層ビルにマッチしたデザインの街路灯
Streertlights designed to compliment the building

19　世界最大規模のクラシック専用ホール
The world's largest, exclusively classic music concert hall

20　アークヒルズ全景
Ark Hills in total perspective

写真提供＝清水行雄
Photos by YUKIO SHIMIZU

取材協力＝森ビル株式会社　加藤吉人
Data Cooperator＝MORI Building Co., Ltd.　YOSHITO KATO

concept of Ark Hills. The very cooperative effort to build up a town on the parts of the developer and area residents, apanning a total of twenty years, is what has made this project a success. Future large-scale urban developments will benefit from the experienced processes covering from the adjustment of regal claims to land to the zoning design that went into this civic development project.

It is of deep significance that the design of "Information City by Advanced Technology" has been accpmplished not by a "Spot Building Development", i.e., sub-dividing and erecting a building on a single block of land but by a "Community-oriented Revitalization of City Covering an Extensive Area".

It is anticipated that Ark Hills will become an establishment toward which people entertain friendly sentiments as an elegant noted place that permits the free exchange of goods, people, and information from around the world by its vigorous management, stimulating the growth of a newer urban culture.

The intention of the environmental design of Ark Hills explicitly indicates suggestions and orientations toward the future, the influencing power of which is almost unfathomable.

1. ランドスケープデザイン
都市計画
タウンスケープ
道路計画
公園計画
広場計画
造園計画
外構計画
etc.

1. Landscape Design
City plannings
Townscapes
Road plans
Park plans
Plazas
Landscapings
Exterior plans
etc.

a. 三井不動産パークシティ新川崎第二番街，セントラルアベニュー
b. 神奈川県川崎市
c. 三井不動産
d. 三井不動産／中島幹夫
e. 鹿島建設建築設計本部:上野卓二，緒方基秀，三木正／三井建設設計部:福本康裕／葛貫武／彫刻=中島幹夫
f. 鹿島建設
g. 五十嵐潔
h. 南北にゆるやかにのびるセントラルアベニュー．暮らす人に優しい環境創りを全体のテーマとした．
i. 舗装材:レンガタイル／モニュメント:御影石／樹種:ケヤキ，クスノキ，カツラ等
j. 鹿島建設建築設計本部

a. PARK CITY SHINKAWASAKI
b. Kawasaki-shi, Kanagawa
c. Mitsui Real Estate Development Co., Ltd.
d. Mitsui Real Estate Development Co., Ltd. : Mikio Naka-jima
e. Kajima Corporation : Takuji Ueno, Motohide Ogata, Tadashi Miki / Mitsui Construction Co., Ltd. : Yasuhiro Fukumoto, Takeshi Tsuzuranuki, Mikio Nakajima
f. Kajima Corporation
g. Kiyoshi, Igarashi
h. The central Avenue that gently extends north and south. A creation of an environment that will provide soft feeling for the residents has been made the theme of the overall design.
i. Pavement material : Brick tile ; Monument : Granite ; Wood : Keyaki / Camphor tree / Katsura tree
j. Kajima Corporation

a. パークシティ新川崎東三番街・プライベートガーデン
b. 神奈川県川崎市
c. 三井不動産
d. 三井不動産／中島幹夫
e. 中島幹夫／三井建設＝福本康裕, 葛貫武　鹿島建設＝
　上野卓二, 緒方基秀　東洋造園土木＝木村紀
f. 三井建設／清水建設
g. 五十嵐潔
h. 子供の遊びを中心とした動的空間と緑に囲まれた静的
　空間の二つの色採られた円形広場の対称性.
i. 磁器タイル／舗石タイル／人工芝／御影石／コンクリー
　ト小タタキ
j. 三井建設設計部建築第二設計室

a. PARK CITY SHINKAWASAKI 3RD BLOCK EAST
　PRIVATE GARDEN
b. Kawasaki-shi, Kanagawa
c. Mitsui Real Estate Development Co., Ltd.
d. Mitsui Real Estate Development Co., Ltd. : Mikio Naka-
　jima
e. Mikio Nakajima, Yasuhiro Fukumoto, Takeshi Tuzuranu-
　ki, Takuji Ueno, Motohide Ogata, Hajime Kimura
f. Mitsui Construction Co., Ltd. ; Shimizu Construction Co.,
　Ltd.
g. Kiyoshi Igarashi
h. Symmetricalness of the two colored circular plazas ; a
　dynamic space principally for children to play around,

on the one hand and a static space surrounded by
green, on the other.
i. Porcelain tile / Pavement tile / artificial lawn / Granite
　/ Dabbed finished concrete
j. Mitsui Construction Co., Ltd.

a. パークシティ新川崎東一番街・プライベートガーデン
b. 神奈川県川崎市
c. 三井不動産
d. 三井不動産／中島幹夫
e. 中島幹夫／三井建設＝福本康裕，葛貫武　鹿島建設＝
　上野卓二，緒方基秀　東洋造園土木＝木村紀
f. 三井建設／熊谷組
g. 五十嵐潔
h. 欅を中心に洋風にまとめたコーナーと，自然石を使った
　自然風庭園との対称の面白さを演出．
i. 磁器タイル／人工芝／玉砂利石洗い出し／コンクリート
　小タタキ／木曽石
j. 三井建設設計部建築第二設計室

a. PARK CITY SHINKAWASAKI 1ST BLOCK EAST
　PRIVATE GARDEN
b. Kawasaki-shi, Kanagawa
c. Mitsui Real Estate Development Co., Ltd.
d. Mitsui Real Estate Development Co., Ltd. : Mikio Naka-
　jima
e. Mikio Nakajima, Yasuhiro Fukumoto, Takeshi Tuzuranu-
　ki Takuji Ueno, Motohide Ogata, Hajime Kimura
f. Mitsui Construction Co., Ltd. ; Shimizu Construction Co.,
　Ltd. ; Kumagai Gumi Co., Ltd.
g. Kiyoshi Igarashi
h. Representation of a strange interest of the symmetry of
　the corner that has been laid out in western style with
　a keyaki in its center relative to the garden of nature
　where natural stones are arranged.
i. Porcelain tile / Artificial lawn / Gravel aggregate
　exposed finish by washing / Dabbed finished concrete
　/ "Kiso" stone
j. Mitsui Construction Co., Ltd.

a. パークシティ新川崎東三番街・アリーナ
b. 神奈川県川崎市
c. 三井不動産
d. 三井不動産／中島幹夫
e. 中島幹夫／三井建設＝福本康裕，葛貫武　鹿島建設＝
　上野卓二，緒方基秀　東洋造園土木＝木村紀
f. 三井建設／清水建設
g. 五十嵐潔
h. 各種のイベントが催される広場．奥にステージ，入口にア
　リーナの存在を表すデザインポール．
i. 磁器タイル／擬石ブロック（階段）
j. 三井建設設計部建築第二設計室

a. PARK CITY SHINKAWASAKI 3RD BLOCK EAST,
　AREA
b. Kawasaki-shi, Kanagawa
c. Mitsui Real Estate Development Co., Ltd.
d. Mitsui Real Estate Development Co., Ltd. : Mikio Naka-
　jima
e. Mikio Nakajima, Yasuhiro Fukumoto, Takeshi Tuzuranu-
　ki, Takuji Ueno, Motohide Ogata, Hajime Kimura
f. Mitsui Construction Co., Ltd. ; Shimizu Construction Co.,
　Ltd.
g. Kiyoshi Igarashi
h. A plaza where various kinds of gathering and entertain-
　ments are held. The sign pole indicating the existence
　of the stage installed in the inmost part and the arena
　at the entrance.
i. Pt / Imitation block (staircase)
j. Mitsui Construction Co., Ltd.

a. 魅力ある道路づくり事業　東口中央通り
b. 神奈川県横浜市
c. 横浜市道路局
d. GK 設計
e. GK 設計
f. 大成道路・松尾工務店建設共同企業体
g. 仲佐写真事務所
h. ウェーブ状の変化ある歩道，路上工作物や標識を統合
　する列柱や共架照明栓で構成した道路空間.
i. 擬石タイル打込み PC 板／白御影／ステンレス／耐候
　性鋼材
j. GK 設計

a. HIGASHIGUCHI CHUO DORI
b. Yokohama-shi, Kanagawa
c. The City of Yokohama Road and Highway Bureau
d. GK Sekkei Associates
e. GK Sekkei Associates
f. Taisei Road Construction Co., Ltd.; Matsuo Komuten Co., Ltd. J.V.
g. T.Nacasa & Partners
h. A footway that has a variation in wavy bending. A street space that is composed of jointly built lighting poles and a row of pillars which comprise integrated road structures and sings.

i. Imitation-stone-placed PC plate / White granite / Stainless steel / Weather proofing steel plate
j. GK Sekkei Associates

a. 日本橋人形町ショッピングモール
b. 東京都中央区
c. 人形町商店街協同組合／東京都中央区役所土木部土
　木課
d. 三枝公一
e. 佐藤康／赤間茂／村越雅行
f. 大成道路／日新舗道建設／コトブキ
g. 佐藤康

h. 「トラディショナルタウン」として，古きよき歴史の中に新し
　い表情が見え隠れし，楽しいイメージをもったショッピング
　モールを提案したものである．
i. 花崗石（白御影・赤御影）／アルミ鋳物／アルミ合金押
　出型材／銅板／ボンデ鋼板
j. サエグサ・都市・建築設計事務所

a. NIHONBASHI NINGYOCHO SHOPPING MALL
b. Chuo-ku, Tokyo
c. Ningyo-cho shopping street Cooperation, Tokyo Chuo
   Ward Office Engineering Dept.
d. Koichi Saegusa
e. Yasushi Sato, Shigeru Akama, Masayuki Murakoshi
f. Taisei Road Construction Co., Ltd. ;   Nisshin Hodo
   Construction Co., Ltd. ;   Kotobuki Seating Co., Ltd.
g. Yasushi Sato
h. A suggestion as to a shopping mall which has a pleasant
   image as a "Traditional town" with contemporary
   expression tangible or intangible against the background of the history of good old days.
i. Granite (white granite and red granite) / Aluminum
   casts / Aluminum alloy extruded profiles / Copper plate
   / Bonderized steel plate
j. Saegusa Urban & Architects Design Office

a. ベル・パークシティ（F.G.H 棟）
b. 大阪府大阪市
c. 三井不動産／カネボウ不動産／デベロッパー三信／進
　和不動産
d. 三井不動産
e. 中島幹夫，大平隆洋，菅原二郎，塙哲夫，林敏夫
f. 東洋造園土木大阪支店
g. 中島幹夫
h.「水と緑の公園都市」をテーマに広場，遊び場，ロビー
　等について総合的な環境デザインを展開．
i. 舗装＝ミッドランドブリック等／彫刻＝白御影石，ブロン
　ズ，大理石モザイク
j. 中島幹夫

a. BELL PARK CITY
b. Osaka-shi, Osaka
c. Mitsui Fudosan Co., Ltd. / Kanebo Fudosan Co., Ltd. /
   Developer Sanshin Co., Ltd. / Shinwa Fudosan, Co., Ltd.
d. Mitsui Real Estate Development Co., Ltd.
e. Mikio Nakajima, Takahiro Ohira, Tetsuo Hanawa, Toshio
   Hayashi
f. Toyo Landscape Constutruction Co., Ltd.
g. Mikio Nakajima
h. With "A park town with water and green" as a theme,
   a comprehensive environmental design of plazas, play-
   grounds, and lobbies has been developed.
i. Pavement (Midland brick, etc.) / Sculpture (white granite / Bronze / Marble mosaic)
j. Mikio Nakajima

a. 麻布十番多目的広場
b. 東京都港区
c. 麻布十番商店街振興組合
d. 上野卓二
e. 都田徹／緒方基秀／野村一雄／飯田清治
f. 鹿島建設
g. 五十嵐潔
h. 新しい街並作りの第一歩として，中心となる道路の広場
　化を計り，今後のショッピングモール化事業の展開に先
　駆けての街作りの核となる広場．
j. 鹿島建設建築設計本部

a. AZABU JUBAN PLAZA
b. Minato-ku, Tokyo
c. Azabu Shotenkai
d. Takuji Ueno
e. Toru Miyakoda, Motohide Ogata, Itsuo Nomura, Seiji
   Iida
f. Kajima Corporation
g. Kiyoshi Igarashi
h. As an initial step to building new rows of stores and
   houses, an attempt has been made at turning the
   central street into a plaza which will play a role of the
   nuclear of the future town building in advance of the
   development of the shopping mall enterprise.
   k. Kajima Corporation

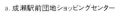

a. 成瀬駅前団地ショッピングセンター
b. 東京都町田市
c. 住宅・都市整備公団東京支社管理部保全第二課
e. 松岡二三夫，上原浩嗣
g. 加藤清仁
h. ステージとシンボルタワーのあるファンシーな買物広場．
　カラフルでクリスタルなファニチャー．
i. レンガ，タイル，ILB，ステージ，シンボルタワー，旗竿，
　ガラスのサイン
j. ベル環境計画事務所

a. NARUSE EKIMAE SHOPPING CENTER
b. Machida-shi, Tokyo
c. Jyutaku Toshi Seibi Kodan
e. Fumio Matsuoka, Hiroji Uehara
g. Kiyohito Kato
h. A fancy shopping plaza that has a stage and a symbol
　tower. Colorful, crystalline furniture.
i. Brick / Tile / ILB / Stage / Symbol tower / Flag pole /
　Sign board of glass
j. Bel Landscape Architectural Design Office

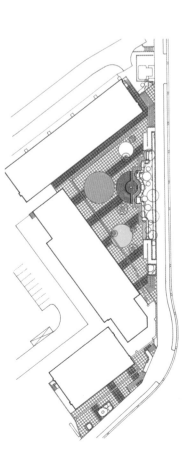

a. NARUSE EKIMAE SHOPPING CENTER
b. Machida-shi, Tokyo
c. Jyutaku Toshi Seibi Kodan
e. Fumio Matsuoka, Hiroji Uehara
g. Kiyohito Kato

a. 七間町名店街並整備
b. 静岡県静岡市
c. 七間町名店街
d. 塩坂博
e. 中村衛
f. 木内建設
g. 中村衛
h. 乱雑な日除けテントから，統一したアーケード，緑を中心とした空間構成化を計った．
i. アルミ，吹付タイル，フッ素樹脂塗料
j. 針谷建築事務所

a. SHICHIKENCHO STREET DESIGN
b. Shizuoka-shi, Shizuoka
c. Shinkokumiai Shichikencho Meitengai
d. Hiroshi Shiosaka
e. Mamoru Nakamura
f. Kiuchi Kensetsu Co., Ltd.
g. Mamoru Nakamura
h. Out of the street of shops and houses with disorderly sunshade tents, an attempt has been made to structure a space with a unified arcade and green placed in its center.
i. Aluminum / Spray-on tile / Fluorine contained resin
j. Harigaya Architects Office

a. 所沢パークタウンショッピングセンター
b. 埼玉県所沢市
c. 住宅・都市整備公団関東支社管理部経営課
e. 仁科孝章, 大山幸弘
g. 加藤清仁
h. 新駅建設に伴う商店街整備. 郊外の緑の豊かさと, 都会的ファッショナブル感覚, 未来感覚の導入.
i. ILB, タイル, 鋼製ゲート, サイン
j. ベル環境計画事務所

a. TOKOROZAWA PARK TOWN SHOPPING CENTER
b. Tokorozawa-shi, Saitama
c. Jyutaku Toshi Seibi Kodan
e. Takaaki Nishina, Yukihiro Oyama
g. Kiyohito Kato
h. A rearrangement of the shopping mall accompanying the construction of the new station. This attempts to introduce the richness of green that matches suburban life, a fashionable sense of urban life, and a sense of the future.
i. ILB / Tile / Steel gate / Sign board
j. Bel Landscape Architectural Design Office

a. 朝日町商店街歩道整備計画
b. 山梨県甲府市
c. 山梨県甲府土木事務所
d. 杉山晃一
e. 星明臣
f. 吉沢建設
g. 古賀修
h. 白・グレー・黒三色のタイルを貼り分け, 山なみを表現. 県鳥のかわせみを絵タイルに焼付けた.
i. INAX・ピエナード＝PB-210-11 (白)／18 (グレー)／20 (黒)
j. ヤシマ

a. SIDEWALK PLAN
b. Kofu-shi, Yamanashi
c. Kofu-public works Office
d. Koichi Sugiyama
e. Akiomi Hoshi
f. Yoshizawa Kensetsu Co., Ltd.
g. Osamu Koga
h. White, grey, and black colored tiles are laid out in assortment expressing the chain of the mountains. The picture of a Kingfisher, the prefecture bird, is baked on a tile.
i. INAX / Pienade / PB-210-11 (white) / 18 (grey) / 20 (black)
j. Yashima Co., Ltd.

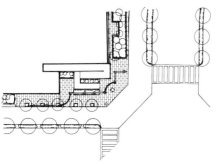
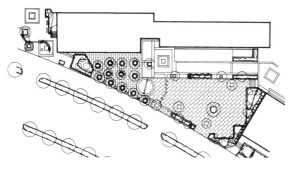

a. 横浜市立大学医学部校舎
b. 神奈川県横浜市
c. 横浜市立大学事務局
d. 広谷敬太郎
e. 松田純男／滝三喜男／藤田泰介　モニュメント＝赤塚
　　昌俊／栄利秋　照明＝石井幹子
f. 熊谷・間・紅梅・小俣 JV ／丸和土建・千代田組 JV
g. 三輪晃久
h. 医学部キャンパスにふさわしい豊かなうるおいのある広
　　場と緑と良好な教育環境を創造する。
i. 花崗石／擬石平板／小タタキ平板　植樹＝クスノキ／
　　ヤマモモ／マテバシイ／クロマツ
j. 松田平田坂本設計事務所横浜支所

a. YOKOHAMA CITY UNIVERSITY SCHOOL OF
   MEDICINE
b. Yokohama-shi, Kanagawa
c. Yokohama City University Administration Office
d. Keitaro Hirotani
e. Sumio Matsuda, Mikio Taki, Taisuke Fujita Monument :
   Masatoshi Akatsuka, Toshiaki Sakai Lighting : Motoko
   Ishii
f. Kumagai Gumi Co., Ltd. ; Hazama-Gumi, Ltd. ; Kobai,
   Omata JV, Maruwa, Chiyoda JV
g. Kohkyu Miwa
h. An attempt at creating rich, charming squares, green,
   and a desirable educational environment worthy of the
   campus of the medical department.
i. Granite / Imitation stone flat plate / Dab finished flat
   plate ; Plant : Camphor tree / Myrica / Makino /
   Black pine
j. Matsuda Hirata Sakamoto Architects Planners Engineers

a. 公園墓地「八景苑」
b. 神奈川県横浜市
c. 神奈川霊園
d. 上野卓二
e. 山本康夫, 長沼寛
f. 鹿島建設
g. 鹿島建設
h. 緑に囲まれた明るく清潔な霊園を設計のテーマとし, 周辺樹林を借景とすると共に, 各所に都市のプラザ的処理を行い, 気軽に来訪できるものとしている.
j. 鹿島建設建築設計本部

a. CEMETERY PARK, "HAKKEIEN"
b. Yokohama-shi, Kanagawa
c. Public Corporation, Kanagawa Reien
d. Takuji Ueno
e. Yasuo Yamamoto, Hiroshi Naganuma
f. Kajima Corporation
g. Kajima Corporation
h. With the concept of a bright, clean cemetery park surrounded by green as a theme of design, the free access of the visitors to the park has been allowed by the provision of urban-like plazas here and there with the peripheral woods standing as their background.
j. Kajima Corporation

a. 長柄東公園
b. 大阪府大阪市
c. 大阪市
d. 藤田好茂
e. 山田直樹，村瀬文彦
f. 宮田・栄興 JV
g. 村瀬文彦
h. 防災通路を兼ねた緑道部に人間の原風景の創造を試みる緩やかな線形と方向性を生む舗装パターン.
i. 陶板／花崗岩
j. 景観設計研究所

a. NAGARA-HIGASHI PARK
b. Nagara-Higasi, Oyodo-ku, Osakacity, Osaka
c. Osaka City Government
d. Yoshishige Fujita
e. Naoki Yamada, Fumihiko Murase
f. Miyata, Eiko J.V.
g. Fumihiko Murase
h. A pavement pattern that will bring forth a gently curved line and directionality is an attempt to create a landscape, that matches the intrinsic human life, in the green road serving both as a disaster-preventive road.
i. China plate / Granite
j. Total Environmental Design Office

a. 神戸総合運動公園中央広場
b. 兵庫県神戸市
c. 神戸市役所
d. 藤田好茂
e. 山田直樹，生田淳一，村瀬文彦
f. 本多工務店 J・B 窪多工業
g. 藤田好茂
h. 運動公園の顔となる広場として花緑水人との出会いがある，シンボル性をもった多機能空間とした．
i. インターロッキング／ステンレス／花崗岩
j. 景観設計研究所

a. MAIN SQUARE OF KOBE ATHLETIC PARK
b. Kobe-shi, Hyogo
c. Kobe city Government
d. Yoshishige Fujita
e. Naoki Yamada, Junichi Ikuta, Humihiko Murase
f. Honda-Koumuten J.B. Kubota-Kogyo
g. Yoshishige Fujita
h. The plaza that represents the athletic park has been made into a symbolized multi-functional space where there will be various encounters of flowers, green, water, and people.
i. Interlocking / Stainless steel / Granite
j. Total Environmental Design Office

a. 二ノ切池公園
b. 大阪府豊中市
c. 豊中市土木部公園緑地課
d. 藤田好茂
e. 大西敏夫／仲純孝　モニュメント＝児玉康兵
f. 飛鳥建設／関造園土木／グレースガーデン／雅園
g. 仲純孝
h. 水が表現する強弱のリズムでもって，水の躍動感を強調した．
i. 花崗岩（白，黒）／木曽石／陶板／人造石（花崗岩，白）／ステンレス
j. 景観設計研究所

a. NINOKIRI-IKE-PARK

b. Toyonaka-shi, Osaka

c. Toyonaka-shi, Doboku-Bu, Koen Ryokuchi-ka

d. Yoshishige Fujita

e. Toshio Onishi, Sumitaka Naka / Monument : Kouhei Kodama

f. Inc. Tobishima Kensetsu ; Inc. Seki-Zoendoboku ; Inc. Guresu-Garden ; Inc. Garen

g. Sumitaka Naka

h. The rhythm expressed by the water is an attempt at emphasizing the vivid motion of water.

i. Granite (white / black) / "Kiso" stone / China plate / Artificial stone (granite white) / Stainless steel.

j. Total Environmental Design Office

a. 喜峯ヶ丘公園
b. 長野県南佐久郡南牧村
c. 南牧村
e. 小山明／原田一二三／山岸和昭
f. 新津組
g. 山岸和昭
h. JR 最高駅『野辺山』の駅前公園で八ヶ岳への畏敬の念と高原の透明感，清らかさをイメージした．
i. 擬石平板（乱張タイプ）／八ヶ岳自然石／佐久石／稲田御影石
j. 公園緑地設計事務所

a. KIBOGAOKA PARK
b. Minamimaki-mura, Minamisaku-gun, Nagano
c. Minamimaki-mura
e. Akira Koyama, Hihumi Harada, Kazuaki Yamagishi
f. Niitsugumi Co., Ltd.
g. Kazuaki Yamagishi
h. The station park of "NOBEYAMA", the JL station built at the highest level has been made to produce an image that will rouse a feeling of awe in Yatsugatake and of transparency and clearness of the plateau.
i. Imitation stone flat plate / Natural stone of Mt. Yatsugatake / "Saku" stone / "Inada" granite
j. Koen Ryokuchi Planning Office

a. 猪名川パークタウンおまつり公園
b. 兵庫県川辺郡猪名川町
c. 三菱地所，竹中工務店，相互住宅
d. 三菱地所土木部
e. 三菱地所土木部
f. 竹中土木，三菱建設
g. 三菱地所猪名川パークタウン事務所
h. 猪名川パークタウン内の自然の池を活用．遊歩道，花見
　 広場を通し住民が自然と触れ合う．
i. 池＝せっ気質施ゆう床タイル／パーゴラ＝鉄骨／健康遊
　 具＝鋼，木製，グリーンテクタ
j. 三菱地所

a. INAGAWA PARK TOWN, OMATSURI KOEN
b. Inagawa-cho, Hyogo
c. Mitsubishi Estate Co., Ltd ; Takenaka Komuten Co.,
   Ltd. ; Sogo Housing Co., Ltd.
d. Mitsubishi Estate Co., Ltd.
e. Mitsubishi Estate Co., Ltd.
f. Takenaka Doboku Co., Ltd., Mitsubishi Construction Co.,
   Ltd.
g. Mitsubishi Estate Co., Ltd.
h. The natural pond within the Inagawa Park Town has
   been utilized and made to serve as a means for the
   residents to come in tough with nature as walking along
   the mall and cherry-blossom-viewing plaza.
i. Pond : Glazed floor tile / Pergola (steel structure) /
   Playthings for health (steel and wood works) / Green
   tecta
j. Mitsubishi Estate Co., Ltd.

a. 泉中央公園
b. 神奈川県横浜市
c. 横浜市
d. 丹羽口憲夫
e. 貝山秀明／モニュメント＝空充秋
f. 横山緑化建設
g. 浦嶋司
h. 泉区の分区記念公園。和泉小次郎の屋敷跡など、歴史
　的題材をテーマにデザインしている。
i. 花崗岩／安山岩／仁加保石／擬木
j. アーク造園設計事務所

a. IZUMI-CENTRAL PARK
b. Yokohama-shi, Kanagawa
c. Yokohama-shi
d. Norio Niwaguchi
e. Hideaki Kaiyama / Monument : Mitsuaki Sora
f. Yokoyama Ryokka Kensetsu
g. Tsukasa Urashima
h. A ward-divisional memorial park of Izumi-ku. The park
　has been designed with the historical objects as a
　theme, such as the remains of the residence of Kojiro
　Izumi.
i. Granite / Andesite / "Nikaho" stone / Imitation wood
j. URC Landscape Architectural Design Office

a. かづさの道
b. 千葉県市原市
c. 住宅・都市整備公団
d. 沖郁二
e. 貝山秀明，小野里宏
f. 富士緑化
g. 貝山秀明
h. ニュータウンの多様な空間をつなぐメインストリート，壮大なイメージを強烈な軸性で表現した，
i. 舗石タイル／アスコン／小舗石／花崗岩
j. アーク造園設計事務所

a. KAZUSA MALL
b. Ichihara-shi, Chiba
c. Housing and Urban Development Corporation
d. Yuji Oki
e. Hideaki Kaiyama, Hiroshi Onozato
f. Fuji Ryokka
g. Hideaki Kaiyama
h. The main street that connects a variety of spaces of the new town. A magnificent image has been produced by providing the street with a powerful axis.
i. Paving block tile / Asphalt concrete / Small paving stone / Granite
j. URC Landscape Architectural Design Office

a. 仙台堀川公園
b. 東京都江東区
c. 江東区
d. 中村誠
e. ゲート他=貝山秀明　古代の砦=彦坂和夫　陶壁=井上猛雄
g. 貝山秀明
h. 仙台堀川公園の始点，流れの始まる水源地帯，歴史の始まるところとしてデザインしている．

i. RC／花崗岩／安山岩／モルタル
j. アーク造園設計事務所

a. SENDAIBORIGAWA PARK
b. Koto-ku, Tokyo
c. Koto-ku
d. Makoto Nakamura
e. Hideaki Kaiyama, Kazuo Hikosaka, Takeo Inoue
g. Hideaki Kaiyama
h. The starting point of Sendaiborigawa Park. The riverhead area where water starts to flow. Designed for a place where history originates.

i. RC / Granite / Andesite / Cement
j. URC Landscape Architectural Design Office

a. 児童公園 「シェルター」
b. 広島県広島市
c. 三井不動産
d. アクラ環境設計／熊本光三
e. 大昌工芸環境デザイン研究所　小池晋弘
f. みずえ緑地
g. 若林誠
h. シックでオーソドックスな感覚の中にも、トップのカラーガラスによる色彩光線での楽しさを表現。
i. スチール／クリンクルガラス／FRP
j. 大昌工芸

a. CHILD PARK "SHELTER"
b. Hiroshima-shi, Hiroshima
c. Mitsui Real Estate Development Co., Ltd.
d. UCLA Urban Design : Mitsuzo Kumamoto
e. Taisho Kogei Co., Ltd., Environmental Design Instittue : Nobuhiro Koike
f. Mizue Ryokuchi Co., Ltd.
g. Makoto Wakabayashi
h. Delight of colored lights that are shed from the stained glass of the shelter top has been expressed in the even tasteful, orthodox feeling of the shelter.
i. Steel / Crinkle glass / Partial "FRP".
j. Taisho Kogei Co., Ltd.

a. 伊勢原市立武道館・桜道公園
b. 神奈川県伊勢原市
c. 伊勢原市
d. 萩原信行　東畑建築事務所東京事務所
e. 萩原信行　東畑建築事務所東京事務所
f. 三井建設・岩崎工務店共同企業体
g. SS 現像所
h. 建物の屋上も含めて敷地のほとんどを公園化し、遊びの
　　舞台装置となるような楽しい環境を提案.
i. 屋根カラーステンレス／外壁コンクリート打放し／50二丁
　　磁器質ラスタータイル
j. 東畑建築事務所東京事務所

a. ISEHARA BUDOKAN
b. Isehara-shi, Kanagawa
c. Isehara City
d. Nobuyuki Hagiwara : Tohata & Associates, Architects
e. Nobuyuki Hagiwara : Tohata & Associates, Architects
f. Mitsui Iwasaki J.V.
g. SS-Genzo shyo
h. A suggestion of a pleasant environment where all the premises including the roof top of the building are turned into a park which will provide a stage setting for play.

i. Roof : Color stainless steel ; External wall : Fair-faced concrete / 50 double size porcelain luster tile
j. Tohata & Associates, Architects

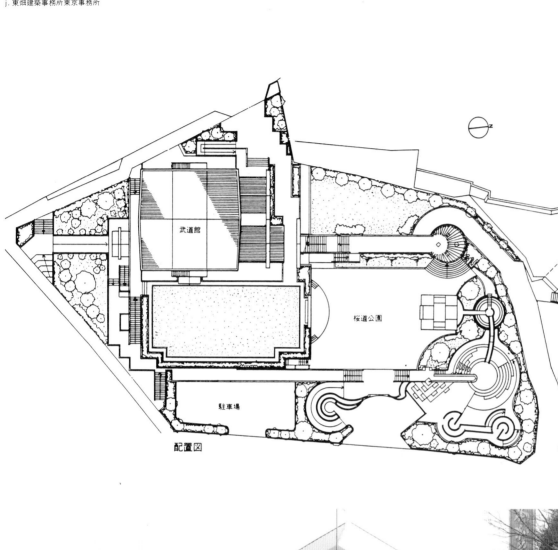

配置図

a. 美術の森緑地
b. 東京都練馬区
c. 練馬区
d. 貝山秀明
e. 貝山秀明
f. 大和ガーデン
g. 貝山秀明
h. 美術館の利用を核としながら日常的にも親しまれる都市
　広場。
i. 陶板（大版タイル）／蛭川御影／木曽石
j. アーク造園設計事務所

a. PARK OF ART MUSEUM
b. Nerima-ku, Tokyo
c. Nerima-ku
d. Hideaki Kaiyama
e. Hideaki Kaiyama
f. Daiwa Garden
g. Hideaki Kaiyama
h. Although the park is basically designed for the visitors
   of the art gallery, the concept intends to create an
   urban plaza that will be genial and accessible for daily
   life purposes, as well.
i. China plate (large size tile) / "Hirukawa" granite /
   "Kiso" stone
j. URC Landscape Architectural Design Office

a. 猪名川パークタウン自然公園
b. 兵庫県川辺郡
c. 三菱地所／竹中工務店／相互住宅
d. 三菱地所土木部
e. 三菱地所土木部
f. 竹中土木／三菱建設
g. 三菱地所猪名川パークタウン事務所
h. 猪名川パークタウン内の自然の池を活用. 遊歩道, 花見
　広場を通し住民が自然と触れ合う.
i. 池＝せっ気質施ゆう床タイル／パーゴラ＝鉄骨／健康遊
　具＝鋼, 木製, グリーンテクタ
j. 三菱地所

a. INAGAWA PARK TOWN, SHIZENKOEN
b. Inagawa-cho, Hyogo
c. Mitsubishi Estate Co., Ltd.; Takenaka Komuten Co.,
　Ltd.; Sogo Housing Co., Ltd.
d. Mitsubishi Estate Co., Ltd.
e. Mitsubishi Estate Co., Ltd.
f. Takenaka Doboku Co., Ltd.; Mitsubishi Construction
　Co., Ltd.
g. Mitsubishi Estate Co., Ltd.
h. The natural pond within the Inagawa Park Town has
　been utilized and made to serve as a means for the
　residents to come in tough with nature as walking along
　the mall and cherry-blossom-viewing plaza.
i. Pond / Glazed tile / Pergola (steel structure) / Play-
　things for health (steel and wood works) / Green tecta
　/ "Nikaho" stone / Imitation stone
j. Mitsubishi Estate Co., Ltd.

a. 江戸川区総合レクリエーション公園区民の森
b. 東京都江戸川区
c. 江戸川区環境促進事業団
d. 高橋清
e. 福室英彦／清水晴一
f. 中里建設
g. 高橋清
h. 江戸川最高峰10mの山に豊かな自然の森を創出，300種の植栽と，デイキャンプのできる施設も設置．
i. 白河石／御影石／小松石／木曽石／レンガタイル／杉丸太／檜角材
j. 創造社

a. EDOGAWA, GENERAL RECREATION PARK "KUMIN NO MORI"
b. Edogawa-ku, Tokyo
c. Edogawa-ku Environment Promotion Enterprise Association
d. Kiyoshi Takahashi
e. Hidehiko Fukumuro, Seiichi Shimizu
f. Nakazato Construction Co., Ltd.
g. Kiyoshi Takahashi
h. Rich, natural woods has been created on the hill of 10 meters high, the highest one in Edogawa-ku. Three hundred kinds of plants have been planted with day camping facilities installed at the same time.
i. "Shirakawa" stone / Granite / "Komatsu" stone / "Kiso" stone / Brick tile / Japanese ceder log / Rectangular timber of Japanese cypress
j. Sozosha Co., Ltd.

a. あすみが丘「創造の杜」公園
b. 千葉県千葉市
c. 土気南土地区画整理組合
d. 山本忠順
e. 清家省二／モニュメント＝内田和孝
f. 東急建設／石勝エクステリア
g. 清家省二
h. 調整池機能を持った地区公園で，子供達が自由に遊べる流れなど，表情豊かな水辺空間を演出した.
i. 磁器質タイル／擬石平板／自然石 (木曽石)
j. L.A.U.都市施設研究所

a. DISTRICT PARK IN ASUMIGAOKA
b. Chiba-shi, Chiba
c. Toke Minami, Land Readjustment Association
d. Tadayuki Yamamoto
e. Shyoji Seike, Monument : Kazutaka Uchida
f. Tokyu Construction Co., Ltd.
g. Shyoji Seike
h. In the district park provided with the function of pondadjustment, a waterside space has been presented which is rich in expression involving a stream where children can freely enjoy play.
i. Porcelain tile / Imitation stone flat plate / Natural stone ("Kiso" stone)
j. L.A.U. Urban Installation Research Institute

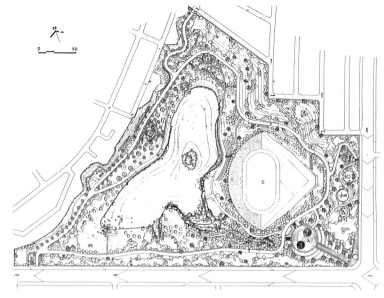

a. 西大和団地造園計画
b. 埼玉県和光市
c. 住宅・都市整備公団関東支社管理部保全第二課
e. 松岡二三夫，小椋雅子，渡辺美枝子
g. 加藤清仁
h. ソフトな曲線が連続，交錯する中にパンチングされた緑と遊具．明るさと広がりと連続感の演出．
i. タイル，平板，コンクリート舗装，ダスト，パーゴラ，鉄製遊具
j. ベル環境計画事務所

a. LANDSCAPE DESIGN FOR NISHIYAMATO DAN-CHI
b. Wako-shi, Saitama
c. Jyutaku Toshi Seibi Kodan
e. Fumio Matsuoka, Masako Ogura, Mieko Watanabe
g. Kiyohito Kato
h. Green and playthings that are spotted amongst the walkways which extend as drawing soft curves and come to across with each other. The intention is an attempt to present the senses of brightness, divergence, and continuation.
i. Tile / Flat plate / Concrete pavement / Dust / Pergola / Playthings made of steel
j. Bel Landscape Architectural Design Office

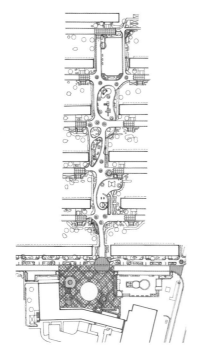

a. 自然の村
b. 長野県和田村
c. 東京都目黒区
d. 門倉行秀
e. 建築＝増子勉／土木＝藤田信行／造園＝佐々木一栄
f. 若築建設
g. 佐々木一栄

h. 霧ヶ峰山系の豊かな自然環境に保養，保健，レクリエーション等の恒久的な拠点づくりを計画．
i. 施設外壁＝カラマツ材／園路舗装材＝インターロッキングブロック／木道＝カラマツ材
j. 創造社

a. NATURAL VILLAGE
b. Wada-mura, Nagano
c. Meguro-ku
d. Yukihide Kadokura
e. Architectur : Tsutomu Masuko, Civil Engineering : Nobuyuki Fujita Landscape Architeture : Kazuei Sasaki
f. Wakachiku Construction Co., Ltd.
g. Kazuei Sasaki

h. The scheme attempts to create a permanent base for preservation of health and recreation in the rich natural environment of the Kirigamine mountain range.
i. External wall of the installation : Japanese larch wood ; Paving material for park walkway : Interlocking block ; Walkway made of split logs : Japanese larch
j. Sozosha Co., Ltd.

a. 鹿島リゾート蓼科高原チェルトの森
b. 長野県茅野市
c. 鹿島リゾート
d. 上野卓二
e. 山本康雄／定塚芳輝／寺島振介／三木正
f. 鹿島建設
g. 鹿島リゾート
h. カラマツやアカマツの樹林を明るく切り開いて創られた庭園風の別荘地とゴルフコース.
j. 鹿島建設建築設計本部

a. TADESHINA KOGEN CERTO NO MORI
b. Chino-shi, Nagano
c. Kajima Resort Corporation
d. Takuji Ueno
e. Yasuo Yamamoto, Yoshiteru Jyozuka, Shinsuke Tera-shima, Tadashi Miki
f. Kajima Corporation
g. Kajima Resort Corporation
h. A garden-fashioned villa site and golf course that have been Laid out through clearing the woods of Japanese larches and Japanese red pines for bright openness.
i. Golf course (18 holes) / Club house / Tennis court / Children's park / Villa place, etc
j. Kajima Corporation

a. 宝塚ゴルフ倶楽部入口部の改修
b. 兵庫県宝塚市
c. 宝塚ゴルフ倶楽部
d. 藤田好夫
e. 大西敏夫
f. 川端造園
g. 大西敏夫
h. 名門ゴルフ場の入口部にふさわしく，風格ある中にも斬新でダイナミックな空間演出を試みた.

i. 丹波石／ケヤキ／ドウダンツツジ／サツキツツジ／コグマザサ
j. 景観設計研究所

a. ENTRANCE OF TAKARAZUKA GOLF CLUB
b. Takarazuka-shi, Hyogo
c. Takarazuka Golf Club (Members)
d. Yoshishige Fujita
e. Toshio Onishi

f. Kawabata Zoen
g. Toshio Onishi
h. An attempt has been made at presenting a space worthy of the entrance of a distinguished golf club that will offer originality and dynamism in the atmosphere of distinctiveness of the club.
i. "Tanba" stone / Keyaki / "Dodan" azalea / azalea / Little bear bamboo grass
j. Total Environmental Design Office

a. 夕やけ広場
b. 東京都北区
c. 北区建設部河川公園課
d. 市田邦治
e. 清家省二
f. 十条製紙＋エバーグリーン
g. 清家省二
h. 新幹線高架下の無機的空間を木のぬくもりで包み, 子供達や老人達のかっこうの遊び空間とした.
i. 木 (フィンランド産・ラップ松)
j. 清家省二

a. YUYAKE-HIROBA
b. Kita-ku Tokyo
c. Kita-ku Kensetsubu Kasenkoen-ka
d. Kuniharu Ichida
e. Shyoji Seike
f. Jyujyo Seisi＋Ever Green
g. Shyoji Seike
h. The design has converted the inorganic space under the elevated railroad of "Shinkansen" into a suitable space for children and the aged by wrapping it in the warmth of wood.
i. Wood (Lapp pine of Finland growth)
j. Shyoji Seike

2. 住環境デザイン

独立住宅

集合住宅

セカンドハウス

これらの外構および造園デザイン

etc.

2. Residential Environmental Design

Houses

Duplexes

Vacation homes and related exterior design projects

etc.

a. コープ野村バードウッド鶴見（シンボルプラザ，中庭）
b. 神奈川県横浜市
c. 野村不動産
d. 戸田建設設計統轄部　吉川雅章
e. 戸田建設設計統轄部　峰岸憲吾
f. 戸田建設
g. 澤田耕造（創芸）／三輪晃久／中村稔（圓写真工房）
h. 泉のモニュメントと虹のゲートは，ここに住む子供達の想
　　い出づくりの舞台装置として提案した．
i. 磁器タイル／御影石／スチール角パイプ
j. 戸田建設

a. NOMURA BIRD WOOD TSURUMI
b. Yokohama-shi, Kanagawa
c. Nomura Real Estate Development Co., Ltd.
d. Toda Construction Co., Ltd. : Masaki Yoshikawa
e. Toda Construction Co., Ltd. : Kengo Minegishi
f. Toda Construction Co., Ltd.
g. Kozo Sawada, Kohkyu Miwa, Minoru Nakamura
h. The monument of spring and the gate of rainbow have
　　been suggested as a stage setting that will be cherished
　　in the heart of the resident children as a reminiscence
　　of their happy childhood.
i. Porcelain tile / Granite / Steel square pipe
j. Toda Construction Co., Ltd.

a. **エルシティ新浦安**
b. 千葉県浦安市
c. 長谷工不動産　他9社
d. 長谷川工務店　金井和修
e. 長谷川工務店　小田義久／山田真五／大栗育夫
f. 長谷川工務店
g. 創芸
h. 新駅を中心とする1700戸の住宅計画に，都市と自然の
　融合をテーマとしてデザインした．
i. インターロッキングブロック／磁器タイル／吹付けタイル
　／ダスト舗装／他
j. 長谷川工務店

a. EL CITY SHIN-URAYASU
b. Urayasu-shi, Chiba
c. Haseko Fudosan Co., Ltd. and Other 9 Companies
d. Hasegawa Komuten Co., Ltd. ;　Kazunobu Kanai
e. Hasegawa Komuten Co., Ltd. Yoshihisa Oda, Shingo
　Yamada, Ikuo Oguri
f. Hasegawa Komuten Co., Ltd.
g. Sogei Co., Ltd.
h. A design with a happy blending of town and nature as
　a theme has been proposed in association with the
　development project of 1700 residences centered
　around the new station.
i. Interlocking block / Porcelain tile / Spray-on tile / Dust
　pavement / Others
j. Hasegawa Komuten Co., Ltd.

a. パーク・シティ金沢八景
b. 神奈川県横浜市
c. 三井不動産 三鋼都市開発 日本製鋼所
d. 翁村和男
e. 森健一／鳥居政治
f. 三井建設 他
g. 読売広告社

h. 公開空地を合わせもった広いオープンスペースと各住棟間に設けた、それぞれが特色のある広場。
i. インターロッキング／花崗岩／カラーアルミ／リブ付コンクリート
j. 三井建設横浜支店

a. PARK CITY KANAZAWA HAKKEI
b. Yokohama-shi, Kanagawa
c. Mitsui Real Estate Development Co., Ltd.　Sanko Toshi Kaihatsu Co., Ltd.　The Japan Steel Works Co., Ltd.
d. Kazuo Omura
e. Kenichi Mori / Masaharu Torii
f. Mitsui Construction Co., Ltd.
g. Yomiuri Kokokusha

h. A wide open space including a vacant lot open to the public and plazas provided in between the apartment buildings, each of which is characterized in their own fashion.
i. Interlocking / Granite / Colored Aluminum / Ribbed concrete
j. Mitsui Construction Co., Ltd.

a. **コスモ志木幸町マンション**
b. 埼玉県志木市
c. リクルートコスモス
d. 上野卓二
e. 寺島振介／三木正／行徳昌則
f. 鹿島建設
g. 三木正
h. 新しいタイプのモールを取り入れながら外部空間全体を
　まとめた．例，歩行者通路，自転車置場等．
i. 舗装＝ILB舗装／壁＝RC打放し／植栽＝マテバシイ，ケ
　ヤキ，ソロ等
j. 鹿島建設建築設計本部

a. **COSMO SHIKI CONDOMINIYM**
b. Shiki-shi, Saitama
c. Recruit Co., Ltd.
d. Takuji Ueno
e. Shinsuke Terashima, Tadashi Miki, Masanori Gyotoku
f. Kajima Corporation
g. Tadashi Miki
h. An integration of the whole external spaces through
　incorporating a new type of mall. For example, wal-
　kways for pedestrians, bicycle yards, and so forth.
i. Pavement : LB pavement ; Wall : Fair-faced RC ;
　Planting : Makino / Keyaki / Solo
j. Kajima Corporation

a. 高見フローラルタウン
b. 大阪府大阪市
c. 住宅・都市整備公団関西支社
d. 藤田好茂
e. 上甫木昭春／生田淳一
f. 内山緑地建設／関西造園土木
g. 生田淳一
h. 基本テーマである花・あかり・水辺の中で特に花をメインとした緑豊かな屋外空間の創出を目指した.
i. 石材(花崗岩)／アイボリーレンガ／インターロッキング／人造石／ステンレス
j. 景観設計研究所

a. TAKAMI FLORAL TOWN
b. Osaka-shi, Osaka
c. Jyutaku Toshi Seibi Kodan, Kansai Branch Office
d. Yoshishige Fujita
e. Akiharu Kamihogi, Junichi Ikuta
f. Uchiyama Green Co., Ltd. ; Kansai Zoen Doboku Co., Ltd.
g. Junichi Ikuta
h. With the brilliance of blossoms as a basic theme, the concept aims at creating an outdoor space rich in green with special emphasis on the flowers arranged on the water side.
i. Stone (granite) / Ivory brick / Interlocking / Artificial stone / Stainless steel
j. Total Environmental Design Office

a. 淀川リバーサイドタウン
b. 大阪府大阪市
c. 住宅・都市整備公団関西支社
d. 藤田好茂
e. 上甫木昭春／仲純孝／生田淳一
f. クラレ緑化産業／東光園緑化
h. 大らかな外部空間の創出及び流れ等の水の積極的な
　導入による水都大阪のイメージの強調.
i. 石材（花崗岩雑石, 赤・黒御影石）／木材（檜, 杉丸太）
　／陶板
j. 景観設計研究所

a. YODOGAWA RIVER SIDE TOWN
b. Osaka-shi, Osaka
c. Jyutaku Toshi Seibi Kodan, Kansai Branch Office
d. Yoshishige Fujita
e. Akiharu Kamihogi, Sumitaka Naka, Junichi Ikuta
f. Kurare Ryokka Co., Ltd.；　Tokoen Green Co., Ltd.
h. A creation of a placid external space and an emphasis
　of the image of the river city by the positive introduction
　of the watery landscape of streams.
i. Stones (miscellaneous black and red granites) / Woods
　(Japanese cypress, Japanese cedar log) / ceramic plate
j. Total Environmental Design Office

a. 泉北城山台二丁団地
b. 大阪府堺市
c. 住宅・都市整備公団関西支社
d. 藤田好茂
e. 仲純孝／村瀬文彦／横田博
f. 西武造園／泉州緑化／朝日興産
g. 仲純孝

h. 現況林を一部保存し，移植による団地内活用と，自然的な曲線の構成により柔らかさを表現した．
i. 花崗岩（サビ）／花崗岩（黒，能勢産）／レンガ（アイボリー）／木材／人造石
j. 景観設計研究所

a. SENBOKU SIROYAMADAI 2-CHO DANCHI
b. Sakai-shi, Osaka
c. Jutaku Toshi Seibi Kodan, Kansai Branch Office
d. Yoshishige Fujita
e. Sumitaka Naka, Fumihiko Murase, Hiroshi Yokota
f. Seibu Zoen, Inc,; Senshu Ryokka, Inc.; Asahi Kosan, Inc.
g. Sumitaka Naka

h. The concept is an attempt to express softness in the landscape by the utilization of the plants which have been transplanted into the residence area with part of the original wood leaving as they are, and by the structure of natural curves.
i. Granite (stain) / Granite (black, from Nose) / Brick (Ivory) / Woods / Artificial stone
j. Total Environmental Design Office

a. パークハイム・狛江
b. 東京都狛江市
c. 三井不動産
d. 添田浩
e. 上野卓二／緒方基秀／飯田清治
f. 鹿島建設
g. 三輪晃久
h. 多摩川の雄大な自然にしっくりと溶け込み，ゆとりとうる
　おいのある外部空間，中庭には，ポケットプラザと水盤を
　配し，床材はボーマナイト舗装て石畳の感じを出した．
j. 鹿島建設建築設計本部

a. PARK HEIM KOMAE
b. Komae-shi, Tokyo
c. Mitsui Real Estate Development Co., Ltd.
d. Hiroshi Soeda
e. Takuji Ueno, Motohide Ogata, Seiji Iida
f. Kajima Corporation
g. Kohkyu Miwa
h. A tasteful external space having latitude which can be
　integrated into the grand nature of the River Tama. In
　the patio, pocket plazas and basins are arranged with
　the flooring expressive of a touch of stone pavement by
　the use of bomanite.
j. Kajima Corporation

植栽参考図

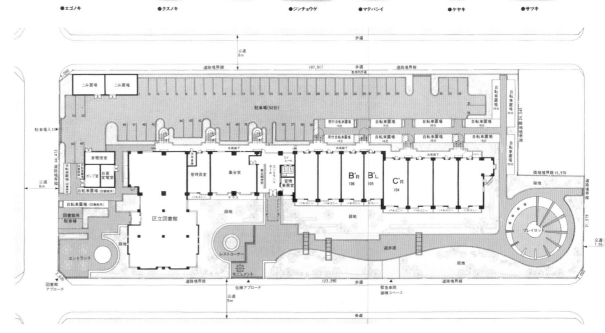

●エゴノキ ●クスノキ ●ジンチョウゲ ●マテバシイ ●ケヤキ ●サツキ

a. ディアハイム赤羽
b. 東京都北区
c. 鹿島建設
d. 石川日出夫
e. 上野卓二／寺島振介／小野寺康夫
f. 鹿島建設
g. 高橋利武建築写真事務所
h. 工業地域に建つ都心型マンション，地域のシンボル―時計塔，特徴的な緑道と子供の遊び場．
i. 舗装＝コンクリートブロック，タイル，洗い出し／植栽＝ケヤキ，クス，雑木類
j. 鹿島建設建築設計本部

a. DEAR HEIME AKABANE
b. Kita-ku, Tokyo
c. Kajima Corporation
d. Hideo Ishikawa
e. Takuji Ueno, Shinsuke Terashima, Yasuo Onodera
f. Kajima Corporation
g. Toshitake Takahashi
h. An urban-type mansion (a high class apartment house) built in an industrial area. The environment comprising a clock tower, which is the symbol of this area, characteristic green-lined walkways and a playground for children.
i. Pavement : Concrete block / Tile / Aggregate exposed finishing by washing ; Planting : Keyaki / Camphor tree / Miscellaneous trees
j. Kajima Corporation

a. 広尾ガーデンヒルズ
b. 東京都渋谷区
c. 住友不動産／三井不動産／三菱地所／第一生命保険相互会社
d. 三菱地所第二建築部／圓堂建築設計事務所
e. 三菱地所第二建築部＝伊藤肇，東條隆郎
f. 広尾ガーデンヒルズ建設工事共同企業体
g. 三輪晃久写真研究所
h. 都心にある集合住宅地の中心施設として，人々が自然と憩う安らぎの場を創ることを目的とした．
i. 花崗岩(赤)／磁器タイル／自然石石積み
j. 三菱地所

a. HIROO GARDEN HILLS
b. Shibuya-ku, Tokyo
c. Sumitomo Realty Development Co., Ltd.; Mitsui Real Estate Development Co., Ltd.; Mitsubishi Estate Company Limited; Daiichi Life Insurance Co., Ltd.
d. Mitsubishi Estate Co., Ltd.: M. Endo Associated Architects & Engineers
e. Mitsubishi Estate Co., Ltd. (Hazime Ito, Takao Tojo)
f. Hiroo Gardenhills Construction JV.
g. Kohkyu Miwa Architectural Photograph Laboratory
h. The concept aims at creating a quiet space, where one can repose with nature, as a central installation of a residential district located in the heart of the metropolis.
i. Granite (red) / Porcelain tile / Natural stone masonry
j. Mitsubishi Estate Co., Ltd.

a. メトロハイツ東陽
b. 東京都江東区
c. 東京都住宅供給公社
d. 日本プレハブ協会
e. 日本プレハブ協会
f. 鹿島建設
g. 川澄建築写真事務所
h. 地下鉄の出入口の上に建つ都心型マンション．モニュメントゲート，自然石のオブジェ等の演出．
i. 舗装＝コンクリートブロック，タイル，アンツーカー／植栽＝武蔵野の雑木材を演出
j. 鹿島建設建築設計本部

a. METRO HEIGHTS TOYO
b. Koto-ku, Tokyo
c. Tokyo Metroporitan Housing Supply Corporation
d. Japan Prefabrication Association
e. Japan Prefablication Association
f. Kajima Corporation
g. Kawasumi Architectual Photograph Office
h. An urban mansion (a high class apartment house) built around the entrance of the subway, which has been accented by the presentation of a monument gate and objects of natural stone.
i. Pavement : Concrete block / Tile / En-tout-cas ; Planting : Representing miscellaneous trees of Musashino area
j. Kajima Corporation

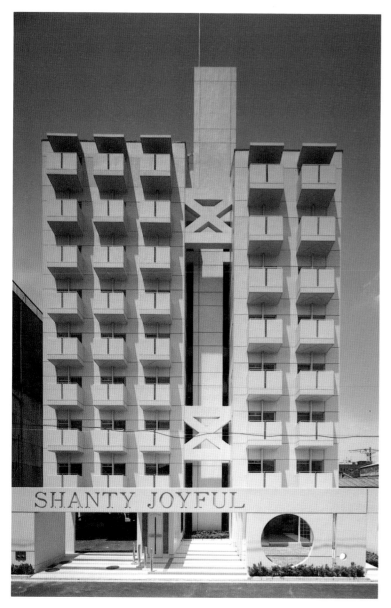

a. シャンティー ジョイフル
b. 大阪府大阪市
c. コシハラ
e. 竹中工務店設計部＝川北英
f. 竹中工務店
g. 大島勝寛
h. 都市型集合住宅，街路に面して，セミパブリックの広場を設け，住環境を保護している．光と影がテーマ．
i. 外壁＝柱梁部分打放しペンキ／壁部分＝タイル／屋根＝アスファルトシングル／床＝タイル
j. 竹中工務店

a. SHANTY JOYFUL
b. Osaka-shi Osaka
c. Koshihara Co., Ltd.
e. Takenaka Komuten Co., Ltd. Building Design Development, Ei Kawakita
f. Takenaka Komuten Co., Ltd.
g. Katsuhiro Oshima
h. An urban housing complex. The installation of a semi-public plaza that fronts the street is an attempt at protecting the living environment. Light and shadow constitute its theme.
i. External wall : fair faced concrete for pillars and beams / Painting ; Walls : Tile ; Roof : Asphalt single ; Floor : Tile
j. Takenaka Komuten Co., Ltd.

a. 淀川リバーサイドタウンさゞなみプラザ
b. 大阪府大阪市
c. 住宅・都市整備公団関西支社
e. 中窪猛
f. 大成建設
g. SS 大阪
h. 統一された集合住宅団地の中にも，明るく暖たかな印象
　の新しい街並み景観を創造．
i. 外壁＝吹付タイル，炉器質タイル打込み／バルコニー＝
　型ガラス，打ち込みタイル
j. 大成建設設計本部

a. "SAZANAMI PLAZA" AT THE YODO RIVER SIDE
　TOWN
b. Osaka-shi, Osaka
c. The Housing and Urban Development Corporation Kansai Branch Office
e. Takeshi Nakakubo
f. Taisei Corporation
g. SS Osaka
h. The concept is an attempt to create such a new landscape of the row of houses and shops in the street that will offer a bright and warm impression even in the unified appearance of the housing complex.
i. External wall : Spray-on tile / Porcelain implanted tile ; Balcony : Shaped glass / Implanted tile
j. Taisei Corporation

a. コンフォート新潟
b. 新潟県新潟市
c. コンフォート有楽
e. 網沢祝栄
f. 大成建設
g. カメラのサタケ（佐武勝也）
h. エグゼクティブの利用にふさわしい格調と日常的な機能
　性を重視したハイグレードな施設．
i. 100角タイル／赤御影石／カラーアルミ
j. 大成建設設計本部

a. COMFORT "NIIGATA"
b. Niigata-shi, Niigata
c. Comfort Yuraku Corporation
e. Norihide Amisawa
f. Taisei Corporation
g. Camera No Satake (Katsuya Satake)
h. A high grade installation that has been designed with special accent on the provision of elegance and daily functions worthy of the use by the executives.
i. 100 square tile / Red granite / Colored Aluminum
j. Taisei Corporation

a. ヴェール久我山
b. 東京都杉並区
c. 秦栄次郎
e. 野村郁夫
f. 大成建設
g. ハットリスタジオ
h. 周辺の住宅環境に調和するスケールでのデザインを心
　掛けました.
i. 磁器小ロタイル／電解2次着色アルミサッシ
j. 大成建設設計本部

a. VERT KUGAYAMA
b. Suginami-ku, Tokyo
c. Eijiro Hata
e. Ikuo Nomura
f. Taisei Corporation
g. Hattori Studio
h. The design is an attempt to develop such a scale that
the building well harmonizes with the surrounding living
environment.
i. Porcelain header tile / Electrolytic secondary colored
aluminum sash
j. Taisei Corporation

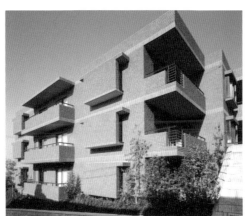

a. 野村向山ヒルズ
b. 愛知県名古屋市
c. 野村不動産
e. 竹中工務店設計部＝古田博司／古川徹
f. 竹中工務店／東海興業共同企業体
g. 光輝／車田写真事務所
h. 外壁材の山型リブ付タイルと, 雁行状の形態により, リズ
　ムと, 陰影と, 高い格調を演出した.
i. 炉器質小ロリブタイル／アルミサッシ／御影石本磨き
j. 竹中工務店

a. NOMURA MUKAIYAMA HILLS
b. Nagoya-shi, Aichi
c. Nomura Real Estate Development Co., Ltd.
e. Takenaka Komuten Co., Ltd., Building Design Department, Hiroshi Furuta, Toru Furukawa
f. Takenaka Komuten Co., Ltd.;　Tokai Kogyo (Joint
Venture)
g. Koki Co., Ltd.
h. Rhythm, shadow, and elegance have been presented by
the adoption of angle-ribbed tiles and the configuration
of a flight of wild geese to the external wall.
i. Porcelain header ribbed tile / Aluminum sash / Polish-
ing finished granite granite
j. Takenaka Komuten Co., Ltd.

a. 藤田観光ヴェルデの森 箱根山ヴィラ
b. 神奈川県足柄下郡箱根町
c. 藤田観光
d. 上野卓二
e. 山本康夫／長沼寛／寺島振介／豊田幸夫
f. 鹿島建設
g. SS東京
h. 自然の樹木を最大限残存させ，建物と自然とが編み出す美しい景観と，建物からの眺望を兼ね供えるように配置したリゾートマンション群．
j. 鹿島建設建築設計本部

a. HAKONEYAMA VILLA, "VERDE-NO-MORI"
b. Hakone-machi, Kanagawa
c. Fujita Tourist Enterprise Co., Ltd.
d. Takuji Ueno
e. Yasuo Yamamoto, Hiroshi Naganuma, Shinsuke Terashima, Yukio Toyoda
f. Kajima Corporation
g. SS Tokyo
h. A group of resort mansions which are so laid out with
   the natural wood left intact to the utmost extent that the
   buildings produce a beautiful landscape in good harmony with the surrounding nature as well as they can
   command a fine view.
j. Kajima Corporation

a. コトー・つきみ野・モンビラージュ
b. 神奈川県大和市
c. デベロッパー三信
d. 長谷川工務店＝橋本百樹
e. 長谷川工務店＝橋本百樹／造園計画＝山本富雄
f. 長谷川工務店
g. 長谷川工務店＝小材雄英

h. 公園を含み約１万３千㎡の緑地を有し、既存樹林（桜）を生かした緑あふれる全体計画とした。
i. 御影石／鉄平石／白河石／木曽石／擬石（御影石）タイル　他
j. 長谷川工務店

a. COTEAU TSUKIMINO MON VILLAGE
b. Yamato-shi, Kanagawa
c. Developer Sanshin Co., Ltd.
d. Hasegawa Komuten Co., Ltd. : Momoki Hashimoto
e. Hasegawa Komuten Co., Ltd. : Momoki Hashimoto ; Landscape Architect : Tomio Yamamoto
f. Hasegawa Komuten Co., Ltd.
g. Hasegawa Komuten Co., Ltd. : Katsuhide Ozai

h. The scheme attempts to present a overall landscape full of green covering a plant area of 13,000 ㎡, inclusive of the park, where the existing wood (cherry trees) has been featured.
i. Granite / Teppei stone / Shirakawa stone / Kiso stone / Artificial stone (granite) tile / Others
j. Hasegawa Komuten Co., Ltd.

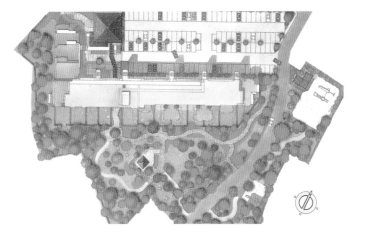

a. 中央測建ビル
b. 北海道札幌市
c. 中央測建
d. 佐藤幸信
e. チーフデザイナー＝中山眞琴
f. 今泉工業
g. 安達治
h. 事務所付住宅にテナント構成という普通さを，統一感ある特異性で存在感を持たせた．
i. 5cm角タイル／ガラスブロック／ステンレス／スチールパイプ
j. スイス設計

a. CHUOSOKKEN BLDG.
b. Chuo-ku, Sapporo-shi, Hokkaido
c. Chuo Sokken, Inc.
d. Yukinobu Sato
e. Chief Designer : Makoto Nakayama
f. Imaizumi Kogyo, Inc.
g. Osamu Adachi
h. A conventional combination of a tenant with a dwelling to which an office is annexed has been provided with uniqueness of architectonic beauty which does not apologize for its existence.
i. 5cm square tile / Glass block / Stainless steel / Steel pipe
j. Suis Planning Design Office

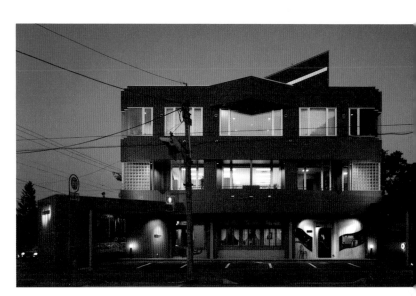

a. CITY SCREEN 1 松下邸
b. 大阪府大阪市
c. 松下俊子
e. 池上俊郎／池上明
f. 谷安組
g. ARC STUDIO＝畑義温
h. 北側道路に対し閉ざし，南面に対して開かれた住居であ
　る．斜めの壁とテラスが，精神空間を象徴する.
i. 外壁＝RC 打放し／開口部＝ステンレスサッシ及びアルミ
　サッシ
j. アーバンガウス研究所

a. CITY SCREEN 1
b. Osaka-shi, Osaka
c. Toshiko Matsushita
e. Toshiro Ikegami, Akira Ikegami
f. Taniyasu-gumi Inc.
g. ARC Studio : Yoshiharu Hata
h. A dwelling closed to the north side street and open to
　the south side. A mental space has been symbolized by
　the oblique wall ends and terraces.
i. External wall : Fair-faced RC / Opening part : Stainless
　steel sash and aluminum sash
j. Urbangauss

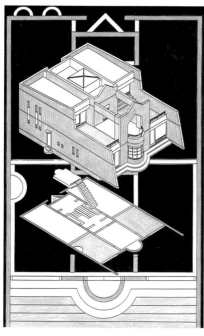

a. CITY SCREEN 5 三宅邸 (増築)
b. 大阪府豊中市
c. 三宅禧尚
e. 池上俊郎／池上明／森井浩一
f. 谷安組
g. URBAN GAUSS
h. 既存住宅の庭を附加されたサンルーム，新築壁面，床の
　ペーブによって，活性化された中庭とした．
i. 外壁＝リシン吹付／アプローチ＝テラゾータイル／開口
　部＝アルミサッシ（アルマイト）
j. アーバンガウス研究所

a. CITY SCREEN 5 MIYAKE RESIDENCE
b. Toyonaka-shi, Osaka
c. Yoshihisa Miyake
e. Toshiro Ikegami, Akira Ikegami, Hirokazu Morii
f. Taniyasu-gumi Inc.
g. Urbangauss
h. A presentation of a patio which has been activated by
　the provision of a sun room to which the garden of the
　existing house has been annexed, newly built walls, and
　floor pavement.
i. External wall : Sprayed lysine ; Approach : terrazo tile ;
　Opening part : Aluminum sash (alumite)
j. Urbangauss

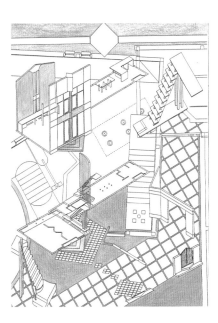

a. CITY SCREEN 5 MIYAKE RESIDENCE
b. Toyonaka-shi, Osaka
c. Yoshihisa Miyake
e. Toshiro Ikegami, Akira Ikegami, Hirokazu Morii
f. Taniyasu-gumi Inc.
g. Urbangauss

a. 高見邸
b. 広島県広島市
c. 高見良
d. 大昌工芸建築設計事務所
e. 新居靖佳／小池晋弘／竹田謙二
f. 増岡組
g. ギンレイ ノオト
h. 市内中心部に位置する為，騒音並びに住宅としての違和感を排除し，内部空間に「ゆとりと快適さ」を集約した．
i. コンクリートタイル貼り／部分的にコンクリート打ち打ち放し／ガラスブロック
j. 大昌工芸

a. TAKAMI PRIVATE RESIDENCE
b. Hiroshima-shi, Hiroshima
c. Ryo Takami
d. Taisho Kogei Co., Ltd.
e. Yasuyoshi Nii, Nobuhiro Koike, Kenzi Takeda
f. Masuoka Construction Co., Ltd.
g. Ginrei Photo
h. The integration of "allowance" and "comfortableness" presented in the internal space of the building is an intention to exclude the noise and the feeling of physical disorder that are most likely to accompany with dwellings located in the heart of the city.
i. Concrete tile laying / Partial fair-faced concrete / Glass block
j. Taisho Kogei Co., Ltd.

a. 川崎邸
b. 北海道札幌市
c. 川崎秀雄
d. 佐藤幸信
e. チーフデザイナー＝中山眞琴
f. 小泉建設
g. 安達治
h. 敷地の狭さから，陸屋根の多くなった北の住宅界にあえて挑戦し，忘れかけたとんがりを表現した．

i. サイディング／長尺カラー鉄板／5cm角タイル／ナラ／ビニールクロス
j. スイス設計

a. KAWASAKI HOUSE
b. Sapporo-shi, Hokkaido
c. Hideo Kawasaki
d. Yukinobu Sato
e. Chief Designer : Makoto Nakayama
f. Koizumi Kensetsu Inc.
g. Osamu Adachi
h. The concept is an attempt at presenting a peaked roof, which has almost escaped living memory, by boldly challenging its application in the northern residence area which has become rich in flat roofs because of the narrow building site.
i. Siding / Long length colored steel sheet / 5cm square tile / Japanese oak wood / Vinyl cloth
j. Suis Planning Design Office

a. S 氏の家
b. 東京都東久留米市
c. S 氏
d. 玉置朝男　ジャパンアートプランニングセンター
e. 設計＝岩渕俊幸
f. 間工務店
g. 大東正巳
h. 家の実体を平面的に構成し，家の虚像を立体的に表現.
i. スチール角パイプ OP ヌリ／スレーター
j. ジャパンアートプランニングセンター

a. S. HOUSE
b. Higashikurume-shi, Tokyo
c. Mr. S
d. Japan Art Planning Center Company Limited : Asao Tamaki
e. Toshiyuki Iwabuchi
f. MASA
g. Masami Daito
h. The substance of the house has been structured in one plane with its virtual image expressed in three dimensions.
i. OP coated steel square pipe / slater
j. Japan Art Planning Center

a. 上野邸
b. 広島県広島市
c. 上野憲昭
d. 佐々木著
e. 佐々木著
g. 西日本写房 (中村実)

h. 大屋根の支持梁が冠木 (かぶき) 門の笠木の象徴性をもつ，車寄せと門兼用の玄関アプローチ．
i. 米松／磁器 (無釉) タイル／ステンレス文字
j. 佐々木著建築設計室

a. UENO HOUSE
b. Hiroshima-shi, Hiroshima
c. Noriaki Ueno
d. Itaru Sasaki
e. Itaru Sasaki
g. Nishi Nihon Shyabo Cld : Minoru Nakamura

h. The bearing beam for the large roof symbolizes the top beam of a roofed gate. The entrance approach that is used as a carriage porch in combination with a gate.
i. Oregon pine / Porcelain (non-glazed) tile / Stainless characters
j. Itaru Sasaki Kensetsu Sekkei Shitsu

a. パレロワイヤル松濤
b. 東京都渋谷区
c. 長谷川工務店
d. 長谷川工務店＝小川雄策
e. 長谷川工務店＝舟橋省一，村上誠
f. 長谷川工務店
g. SS 東京・島尾望／創芸・松吉康司／東京 DP・吉野改治
h. 「和と洋を超えた美しさ」を，基本コンセプトとした．外人向賃貸マンション．
i. ニューインド砂岩／コールテン鋼／黒御影石／大理石
j. 長谷川工務店

a. PALAIS ROYAL SHOHTOH
b. Shibuya-ku, Tokyo
c. Hasegawa Komuten Co., Ltd.
d. Hasegawa Komuten Co., Ltd. : Yusaku Ogawa
e. Hasegawa Komuten Co., Ltd. : Seiichi Funabashi, Makoto Murakami
f. Hasegawa Komuten Co., Ltd.
g. SS Tokyo Co., Ltd. : Nozomu Simao ; Sogei Co., Ltd. : Koji Matsuyoshi ; Tokyo DP Co., Ltd. : Kaiji Yoshino
h. The basic concept is an attempt at realizing "the beauty that stands aloof from both Japanese style and western style". A mansion for lent for foreigners.
i. New Indian sandstone / Cor-ten steel / Black granite / Marble
j. Hasegawa Komuten Co., Ltd.

3.公共・オフィス環境デザイン

福祉施設
医療施設
交通施設
庁舎
銀行
学校
博物館
ビジネスビル
これらの外構および造園デザイン
etc.

3. Public & Office Environmental Design

Welfare and social facilities
Clinics, Motor vehicle departments
Municipal offices
Banks
Schools
Museums
Business buildings and related outdoor design and landscapings
etc.

a. 東洋英和女学院短期大学校舎等
b. 神奈川県横浜市
c. 東洋英和女学院
d. 三菱地所第一建築部
e. 三菱地所株式会社第一建築部 (新居仁)
f. 大林組, 鹿島建設, 清水建設共同企業体
g. 航空写真＝SS 東京　建物写真＝川澄建築写真事務所
h. 自然環境との調和とキリスト教主義の教育実践の場に
　 ふさわしい落ち着きのある清楚な建物とした.
i. 外壁＝コンクリート打放し, 磁器タイル, アルミサッシ
j. 三菱地所

a. TOYO EIWA JYOGAKUIN JUNIOR COLLEGE
　 BUILDINGS
b. Yokohama-shi, Kanagawa
c. Toyo Eiwa Jyogakuin
d. Mitsubishi Estate Co., Ltd.
e. Mitsubishi Estate Co., Ltd. Hitoshi Arai
f. Ohbayashi, Kajima, Shimizu JV
g. SS Tokyo ; Kawasumi Architectural Photograph Office
h. The Junior College Buildings have been afforded calm,
　 neat atmosphere worthy of the place where the campus
　 well harmonizes with nature and the education through
　 Christianity is put to practice.
i. External wall : Fair-faced concrete / Porcelain tile /
　 Aluminum sash
j. Mitsubishi Estate Co., Ltd.

a. 大東文化大学東松山キャンパス
b. 埼玉県東松山市
c. 大東文化学園
d. 建築モード研究所＝大森勝美／鹿島建設＝上野卓二
e. 山本康雄／川畑了／寺島振介／豊田幸夫
f. 開発造成工事＝鹿島建設／建築工事＝鹿島建設，飛鳥建設，フジタ工業共同企業体
g. SS 東京＝末広久詔
h. 調整池を風景として憩の場として活用する等，自然地形を生かした機能的で豊かな環境とした.
j. 鹿島建設建築設計本部

a . DAITOBUNKA UNIVERSITY HIGASHIMAT-
   SUYAMA CAMPUS
b. Higashimatsuyama-shi, Saitama
c. Daitobunkagakuen Scholastic Foundation
d. Kenchiku Mode Kenkyujyo Co., Ltd. : Katsumi Omori ;
   Kajima Corporation : Takuji Ueno
e. Yasuo Yamamoto ; Ryou Kawabata / Shinsuke Terashima ; Yukio Toyoda
f. Kajima Corporation & Kajima, Tobishima, Fujita JV
g. SS Tokyo Hisaaki Suehiro
h. The scheme is an attempt at creating a functional,
   affluent environment by making full use of the configuration of natural ground, i.e., utilizing the pondage as a
   landscape for the place of recreation and relaxation.
i. Memorial library / Memorial hall / Comprehensive gym-
   nasium / School building / Laboratory building / Over
   bridge / Others
j. Kajima Corporation

a. 姫路獨協大学
b. 兵庫県姫路市
c. 獨協学園
d. 由利忠雄
e. 落合正明／河津行隆
f. 大林組神戸支店
g. ナトリ工房
h. ゆるやかな南斜面の校地に三つの違った高さの広場を
　中心に展開するキャンパス空間を構成した．
i. 大理石／花崗岩／インターブロッキングブロック／コンク
　リート打放し
j. 大林組東京本社一級建築士事務所

a. HIMEJI DOKKYO UNIVERSITY
b. Himeji-shi, Hyogo
c. Dokkyo-Gakuen
d. Tadao Yuri
e. Masaaki Ochiai, Yukitaka Kawazu
f. Ohbayashi-gumi, Ltd.
g. Natori-kobo
h. A campus space which extends around the three plazas different in height has been constructed on the campus ground cleared on an easy south slope.
i. Marble / Granite / Interblocking block / Fair-faced concrete
j. Ohbayashi-gumi, Ltd.

a. 創造社デザイン専門学校
b. 大阪府大阪市
c. 創造社学園
e. 竹中工務店設計部＝鎌谷憲彦／藤原時一郎
f. 竹中工務店
g. 大島勝寛
h. 現代社会のデザイン活動にダイナミックに係わっていこう
　　とする学園の方針の表象.
i. ラスタータイル／熱線反射ガラス／アルミ
j. 竹中工務店

a. SOZOSHA COLLEGE OF DESIGN
b. Osaka-shi, Osaka
c. Sozosha College of Design
e. Takenaka Komuten Co., Ltd., Building Design Depart-
　　ment Norihiko Kamatani, Tokiichiro Fujiwara
f. Takenaka Komuten Co., Ltd.
g. Katsuhiro Oshima
h. A representation of the campus policy with which the
　　campus attempts to dynamically concern themselves
　　with the design activities of the contemporary society.
i. Luster tile / Heat ray reflecting glass / Aluminum
j. Takenaka Komuten Co., Ltd.

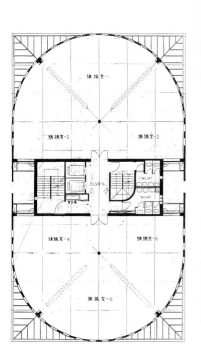

a. 加世田市立加世田小学校
b. 鹿児島県加世田市
c. 加世田市
e. 石本建築事務所
f. 前田組／東建設
h. 色彩や空間の形に変化を与え，教育の場としてだけでな
  く，子供達の生活の場として学校を捉えた，
i. 外壁＝コンクリート打放し CL ／壁＝米松合板 OS ／床＝
  寄木フロアーパーケット
j. 石本建築事務所

A. KASEDA-SHI KASEDA SHOGAKKO
b. Kaseda-shi, Kagoshima
c. Kaseda-shi
e. Ishimoto Architectural & Engineering Firm, Inc.
f. Maeda-Gumi Co., Ltd. ; Higashi-Kensetsu Co., Ltd.
h. The concept is an attempt at seeing school in the light
  of living environment of children rather than of educational facilities by giving variation in coloration and
  space.
i. External wall : CL on fair-faced concrete ; Wall : OS on
  oregon pine ; Floor : Parketry floor.
j. Ishimoto Architectural & Engineering Firm, Inc.

a. 聖ヨゼフ学園
b. 神奈川県横浜市
c. 贖罪会
e. 千本木隆芳
f. 大成建設
g. 大成建設
h. 小さい敷地に効率良く外部環境との接点に緑を設け,
　建物はあくまで白く, 雰囲気作りを考えた.
i. 外壁＝白磁器タイル／内部空間＝モザイクタイル, テッセ
　ラタイル
j. 大成建設設計本部

a. ST. JOSEPH SCHOOL
b. Yokohama-shi, Kanagawa
c. Shokuzaikai
e. Takayoshi Senbongi
f. Taisei Corporation
g. Taisei Corporation
h. The concept is an attempt to produce aome atmosphere
　by efficiently providing green in the restricted site at
　the point of contact between the site and the external
　environment with the building painted as white as it can
　be.
i. Wall : White porcelain ; Interior : Mosaic tile / Artificial
　tile
j. Taisei Corporation

a. 大阪学院短期大学
b. 大阪府吹田市
c. 大阪学院大学
d. 浅輪誠
e. 上野卓二／都田徹／野村一雄／又平清美
f. 鹿島建設
g. 銀総
h. 噴水とアートウォールをもつ, ソフトでお洒落な感覚のカレッジ. 狭い敷地の中での多様な演出とハイグレードな仕上げ内容が建物と一体となって, 斬新な中にも親しみのある外部空間を創り出している.
j. 鹿島建設建築設計本部

a. OSAKA GAKUIN JUNIOR COLLEGE
b. Suita-shi, Osaka
c. Osaka Gakuin University
d. Makoto Asawa
e. Takuji Ueno, Toru Miyakoda, Itsuo Nomura, Kiyomi Matahira
f. Kajima Corporation
g. Ginso Co., Ltd.
h. A soft-touch, chic college that has a fountain and out walls. The diversified presentation of the building in the narrow site and the contents of the sophisticated finishing coupled with the building have created an external space that has a friendly feeling even in its novel design.
j. Kajima Corporation

g. 川澄建築写真事務所

富士山を背にした緑豊かな研究所．芝と針葉樹主体の緑の演出．

a. 中外製薬御殿場研究所
b. 静岡県御殿場市
c. 中外製薬
d. 羽生昌弘
e. 上野卓二／寺島振介／小野寺康夫
f. 鹿島建設

g. 川澄建築写真事務所
h. 富士山を背にした緑豊かな研究所．既存林の保存と研究所にふさわしい芝と針葉樹主体の緑の演出．
i. 舗装＝コンクリートブロック，アスファルト／樹木＝メタセコイア，ヒマラヤシーダ
j. 鹿島建設建築設計本部

a. CHUGAI PHARMACEUTICAL COMPANY, FUJI
   GOTENBA RESEARCH LABORATORY
b. Gotenba-shi, Shizuoka
c. Chugai Pharmoceutical Company
d. Masahiro Hanyu
e. Takuji Ueno, Shinsuke Terashima, Yasuo Onodera

f. Kajima Corporation
g. Kawasumi Architectural Photograph Office
h. A laboratory surrounded by rich green, standing with its
   back against Mt. Fuji. The landscape is represented by
   the preserved existing wood, the lawn matching the
   laboratory, and the green principally consisting of

needle leaf trees.
i. Pavement : Concrete block / Asphalt ; Trees : Metase-
   quoia
j. Kajima Corporation

a. 小国町役場

b. 山形県西置賜郡

c. 小国町

e. 本間利雄設計事務所＋地域環境計画研究室

f. 佐藤工業・安藤建設特別共同企業体

g. SS 東北 菅雅昭

h. カリヨンのあるタワー，庁舎，樹木に囲まれた町民広場を都市と山村の交錯する場とした．

i. 砂利洗い出し／磁器質タイル／樹木は地区内から集められたブナ／ヤマモミジ等

j. 本間利雄設計事務所＋地域環境計画研究室

a. OGUNI TOWN HALL

b. Nishi-Okitama-gun, Yamagata

c. Oguni-machi

e. Toshio Honma & Associates

f. Sato Kogyo Co., Ltd. ; Ando Construction Co., Ltd., JV

g. SS Tohoku ; Masaaki Kan

h. The tower with a carilon, Government building, and towns folk square surrounded by trees have been made a place where the atmosphere of a city mingles with that of a mountain village.

i. Gravel scrubbed finish / Porcelain tile ; Trees : Beech / Maple / Others

j. Toshio Honma & Associates

a. 東京ネットワークセンター
b. 東京都多摩市
c. 第二電電
e. 竹中工務店設計部　臼井真／塩原敏男／監理者＝日本設計事務所
f. 熊谷組，竹中工務店，清水建設共同企業体
g. 三輪晃久写真研究所
h. 白い壁面と反射ガラスの構成による鋭いかたちで"先端通信技術のイメージ"を表現した．
i. アルミ／熱線反射ガラス／コンクリート／フッ素樹脂系吹付タイル
j. 竹中工務店

a. TOKYO NETWORK CENTER
b. Tama-shi, Tokyo
c. Daini-denden Inc.
e. Takenaka Komuten Co., Ltd., Building Design Department Makoto Usui, Toshio Shiobara
Nihon Architects, Engineers & Consultants, Inc.
f. Kumagai Gumi ; Takenaka Komuten ; Shimizu Contruction V
g. Kohkyu Miwa Architechtural Photograph Laboratory
h. The image of an advanced communication technology has been expressed with a sharp configuration composed of white wall sides and reflecting glass.
i. Aluminum / Hear ray reflecting glass / Concrete / Fluorine contained resin spray-on tile
j. Takenaka Komuten Co., Ltd.

a. 千代田化工建設子安総合研究所
b. 神奈川県横浜市
c. 千代田化工建設
d. 福本行
e. 上野卓二／都田徹／加藤敬
f. 鹿島建設
g. 川澄明男
h. 21世紀の研究所をめざし，緑豊かな外部空間のデザイン
を行った．この地域では珍しく緑が多くなった．
i. ケヤキ／サクラ／ニレ／ハナミズキ／タイル／インターロ
ッキングブロック
j. 鹿島建設建築設計本部

a. GENERAL LABORATORY FOR CHIYODA
CHEMICAL ENGINEERING & CONSTRUCTION
b. Yokohama-shi, Kanagawa
c. Chiyoda Chemical Engineering & Construction Co., Ltd.
d. Tsuyoshi Fukumoto
e. Takuji Ueno, Tooru Miyakoda, Kei Kato
f. Kajima Corporation
g. Akio Kawasumi
h. The design is an attempt to create an external space
rich in green, aiming at a laboratory of the 21 th
century. (Green has unexpectedly become rich in this
region.)
i . Keyaki / Cherry / Elm / Dogwood / Tile / Interlocking
block
j. Kajima Corporation

a. 栄町立中央小学校
b. 新潟県栄町
c. 米山建築設計事務所
d. 刈屋剛／相馬成男
e. 刈屋剛
f. 味方硝子
g. 刈屋剛
h. 音楽をテーマに，それらの音色をさまざまな線の構成で
　表現した．
i. 強化ガラス／サンドブラスト仕上
j. アスカデザイン室

a. SAKAE CHYORITSU CHUO SHOGAKKO
b. Sakae-machi, Niigata
c. Yoneyama Inb.
d. Go Kariya, Shigeo Soma
e. Go Kariya
f. Ajikata Garasu Co.
g. Go Kariya
h. With music as a theme, its tones have been expressed
   by the structure of various kinds of lines.
i. Tempered glass / Sand blast finish
j. Asuka Inc.

a. 館林市赤羽公民館勤労青少年ホーム
b. 群馬県館林市
c. 館林市役所
d. 渡辺益男
e. 板川敏治／松村一幸／林啓
f. 小曽根建設
g. フジタマン写真事務所
h. 地域社会との融和と東西に設けた軸線による4ブロック
　の独立性の表現をテーマとしている．
i. 外壁＝炉器質タイルイギリス貼り／カーテンウォール熱線
　反射ガラス
j. 渡辺建築事務所

a. TATEBAYASHI COMMUNITY CENTER
b. Tatebayashi-shi, Gunma
c. Tatebayashi City Office
d. Masuo Watanabe
e. Toshiharu Itagawa / Kazuyuki Matsumura / Kei Hayashi
f. Ozone Kensetsu Co., Ltd.
g. Man Photo Office
h. The theme of this community center attempts to
   express the happy blending of the center building with
   the local society, and the independency of the four
   blocks divided by an axis provided east and west.
i. Wall : Porcelain tile (English laying) / Curtain wall (heat
   ray reflecting glass)
j. M. Watanabe Architects & Engineers Co., Ltd.

a. 太陽神戸銀行六甲支店
b. 兵庫県神戸市
c. 太陽神戸銀行
e. 竹中工務店設計部　井本由之
f. 竹中工務店
g. 野竹満
h. ファサードは，おおらかな楕円曲面を描きながら，ネガティヴな緩衝領域をかたち作り，街並とやさしく接している．基台には，この地域の記憶の再生として六甲の石積を用いた．
i. 外壁＝アルミパネル，打放し化粧コンクリート，ガラスブロック，炉器質スクラッチボーダータイル，茶糸花崗岩（御影石）積／舗装＝黒花崗岩ジェット仕上／植栽＝クスノキ他
j. 竹中工務店

a. THE TAIYO KOBE BANK CO., LTD. ROKKO BRANCH
b. Kobe-shi, Hyogo
c. The Taiyo Kobe Bank Co., Ltd.
e. Takenaka Komuten Co., Ltd. Building Desing Department Yoshiyuki Imoto
f. Takenaka Komuten Co., Ltd.
g. Mitsuru Notake
h. The facade of the building, generating a serene oval curved surface, configures a buffer zone, gently interfacing with the row of stores and houses on the street. As a means to recall the memory of the district, maisonry of Rokko has been used.
i. External wall : Aluminum panel / Fair-faced decorative concrete / Glass block / Porcelain scratch border tile / Granite laying ; Pavement : Black granite jet finish ; Planting : Camphor tree and others
j. Takenaka Komuten Co., Ltd.

a. 日本テレビ生田スタジオ
b. 神奈川県川崎市
c. 日本テレビ放送網
d. 設計監修＝三菱地所
e. 橋本緑郎／塚田哲也
f. 大成建設
g. 根本昇
h. テレビドラマ制作のスタジオ，全館が創造の場としての空間を念頭に設計されている．
i. 45，二丁リブ付ラスタータイル／熱線反射／ガラス／アルミサッシ
j. 大成建設設計本部

a. NTV IKUTA STUDIO
b. Kawasaki-shi, Kanagawa
c. Nippon Television Network Corporation
d. Mitsubishi Estate Company Limited
e. Rokuro Hashimoto, Tetsuya Tsukada
f. Taisei Corporation
g. Noboru Nemoto
h. A studio for production of TV dramas. The whole studio has been constructed by the design with a space being as a place of creation on mind.
i. 45.2 T ribbed luster tile / Heat ray reflecting glass / Aluminum sash
j. Taisei Corporation

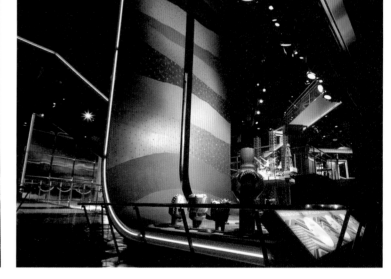

a. ガスの科学館
b. 東京都江東区
c. 東京ガス
d. 総合プランナー=吉原順平／建築環境設計=古見修一
　／アートディレクター=稲垣博／プランナー=福島みち子
e. デザイナー=鏡味賢二，石井康一，関俊郎，吉山透，
　江蔵紀一／グラフィックデザイナー=原田豊，宮野哲也
　／造形デザイナー=中山隆
f. 総合監理=電通／プロダクション=乃村工藝社
g. 大東正巳

h. 施設全体を「ガスの旅」と設定し，人・物との出逢いと
　期待感の連続のある空間構成を目指した．
i. メンブレン (LNG タンク内装材)／LNG 気化器・ガス配管
j. 関俊郎

a. GAS SCIENCE CENTER
b. Koto-ku, Tokyo
c. Tokyo Gas Co., Ltd.
d. Junpei Yoshiwara, Shuichi Furumi, Hiroshi Inagaki
e. Kenji Kagami, Koichi Ishii, Toshiro Seki, Toru Yo-
shiyama, Norikazu Ezo, Takashi Nakayama
f. Total Supervisor : Dentsu ; Production : Nomura Display
g. Photographer : Masami Daito

h. The concept, through setting up the whole facilities into
"Trip for gas", aims at constructing a space which
will allow the visitors to entertain continuous expectations for encountering people and things.
i. Membrane (interior material for LNG tank) / LNG
vaporizer / Piping for gas
j. Toshiro Seki

a. **ガスの科学館**
b. 東京都江東区
c. 東京ガス
d. ガスの科学館企画グループ（総合プロデュース＝吉原順平）
e. 古見修一（SD設計室），潮田宏平，河野晴彦（大成建設設計本部），展示設計＝電通，乃村工藝社
f. 大成建設
g. 大成建設

h. "ガスの旅"をテーマに，展示と建築の一体化を目指したコミュニケーションメディアとしての空間．
i. 屋根＝ステンレス折版丸馳 I 型ボルトレス工法／壁＝ステンレス折版ルーフデッキ（横張）
j. 大成建設設計本部

a. GAS SCIENCE CENTER
b. Koto-ku, Tokyo
c. Tokyo Gas Co., Ltd.
d. "Gas Science Center" Project-team : Total Produce : Junpei Yoshiwara
e. SD Planning Co., Ltd. : Shuichi Furumi / Taisei Corporation : Kohei Ushioda, Haruhiko Kono / Dentsu Incorporated ; Nomura Display Co., Ltd.
f. Taisei Corporation
g. Taisei Corporation

h. A space created as a communication medium where the concept, with "Trip for gas" as the theme, aims at uniting the display with the architecture.
i. Roof : Stainless sheet I-type boltless technique ; Wall : Stainless steel sheet roof deck
j. Taisei Corporation

a. 丸紅大阪本社ビル
b. 大阪府大阪市
c. 丸紅
d. 三菱地所第一建築部
e. 三菱地所第一建築部＝内川正人，松村富健
f. 竹中工務店，大成建設，鹿島建設，清水建設　共同
　企業体
g. 大島勝寛
h. 都心の中にオアシスの景観を演出し，街区周辺の環境
　整備に努めた．
i. 床＝花崗岩ジェットバーナー仕上／コンクリート洗い出し
　仕上
j. 三菱地所

a. MARUBENI OSAKA HEAD OFFICE
b. Osaka-shi, Osaka
c. Marubeni Co., Ltd.
d. Mitsubishi Estate Company Limited
e. Mitsubishi Estate Company Limited, Masato Uchikawa,
　Tomio Matsumura
f. Takenaka, Taisei, Kajima, Shimizu JV
g. Katsuhiro Oshima
h. The concept is an attempt to represent a landscape of
　an oasis in the heart of the city, and to put the environ-
　ment around the block concerned in good condition.
i. Floor : Jet-burner-finished granite / Aggregate exposed
　finishing of concrete by washing
j. Mitsubishi Estate Company Limited

a. 浜松プレスタワー
b. 静岡県浜松市
c. 静岡新聞社／山六総業／土屋土地開発／ダルマヤ
e. 水嶋隆二／倉岡誠一／角田隆彰
f. 大成建設
g. センターフォト
h. 半楕円の筒をナイフですっぱりと切った潔いスタイル．発展する浜松駅前を象徴するランドマークの実現．
i. 外壁＝アルミカーテンウォール（風紋模様）／プラザ床＝花崗石模様貼
j. 大成建設設計本部

a. HAMAMATSU PRESS TOWER
b. Hamamatsu-shi, Shizuoka
c. Shizuoka Shimbun Co., Ltd. & Others
e. Ryuji Mizushima, Seiichi Kuraoka, Takaaki Tsunoda
f. Taisei Corporation
g. Center Photo Co., Ltd.
h. The tower stands in a gallant style looking like a semielliptic cylinder cut with a bald stroke with a knife. The realization of a land mark which symbolizes the developing station-front of the "Hamamatsu-cho" station.
i. External wall : Aluminum curtain wall (wind-wrought pattern on the sands) ; Plaza floor : Granite pattern flooring
j. Taisei Corporation

a. 吉本ビルディング
b. 大阪府大阪市
c. 吉本ビルディング
e. 竹中工務店設計部　小川清一，仲井領，野村充
f. 竹中工務店
g. 村井修

h. 外観はモノトーンを基調色とし，敷地なりの水平曲面と高層棟の垂直に伸びた曲面で構成している。
i. 45，二丁掛施釉磁器タイル／アルミメタリック焼付塗装／ガラス／花崗岩／ステンレスバフ
j. 竹中工務店

a. YOSHIMOTO BUILDING
b. Osaka-shi, Osaka
c. Yoshimoto Building Co., Ltd.
e. Takenaka Komuten Co., Ltd., Building Design Department Seiichi Ogawa, Kaname Nakai, Mitsuru Nomura
f. Takenaka Komuten Co., Ltd.
g. Osamu Murai
h. The building image is composed by the horizontally curved surface conforming to the geometry of the site and the curved surface extending in the vertical direction of the high-rise building with a monotonic color as the keynote one of the external appearance.
i. 45 double size glazed porcelain tile / Aluminum metallic baking painting / Glass / Granite / Stainless steel buff finished
j. Takenaka Komuten Co., Ltd.

a. 日本生命千駄ケ谷ビル
b. 東京都渋谷区
c. 日本生命保険相互会社
e. 田辺詔二郎／鈴木智子
f. 大成建設
g. 野口毅　根本写真工芸社
h. 地下に掘り下げたサンクンガーデンは，接地性の良い明るい地下居室と，通りに広がりを生み出している．
i. 外壁＝45，二丁タイル／サンクンガーデン床＝色骨材と顔料による＝地なし砂利洗出し
j. 大成建設設計本部

a. NIHON SEIMEI SENDAGAYA BUILDING
b. Shibuya-ku, Tokyo
c. Nihon Seimei
e. Shojiro Tanabe, Tomoko Suzuki
f. Taisei Corporation
g. Takashi Noguchi
h. The sunken garden that has been dug down in the ground has brought forth a bright basement living-room with good grounding ability and afforded an expanse to the street.
i. External wall: 45 double size tile; Floor of sunken garden: Monolithic aggregate exposed finishing by washing by the use of colored aggregate and pigment.
j. Taisei Corporation

a. 中日友好囲棋会館
b. 北京市天壇東路
c. 日中経済協会／日本棋院
e. 野呂一幸
f. 大成建設
g. 大成建設
h. 天壇公園の屋根との調和，日本的な外観と中国的インテリアの演出を基本コンセプトとした．
i. 中国産大理石／フッ素樹脂焼付鋼板／アルミ断熱サッシ／複層ガラス
j. 大成建設設計本部

a. GO-CLUB IN MEMORY OF THE FRIENDSHIP BETWEEN CHINA AND JAPAN
b. Tientan-donglu Street Beijing-shi, China
c. Japan-China Association on Economy and Trade ; The Nihon Kiin
e. Kazuyuki Noro
f. Taisei Corporation
g. Taisei Corporation
h. The basic concept is an attempt at establishing a harmony between the building and the roof of Tien Tan Gong Yuan (park), and presentation of an external appearance of a Japanese version and an interior of a Chinese version.
i. Marble from China / Fluorine contained resin baking paint on steel plate / Aluminum thermal insulating sash / Double layer glass
j. Taisei Corporation

a. 松本木工館
b. 長野県松本市
c. 松本木工団地事業協同組合
d. GK設計　西沢健／朝倉則幸
e. 渡和由／田村賢治／岩崎耕一
f. 北野建設
g. 岩為
h. 木工家具産業を基盤とするDIY研修展示施設．鉄と木の構成で開放的なショーケースの表情を持つ．
i. カラマツ大断面集成材／スチール／セメント中空押出成型板／アルミ
j. GK設計

a. MASUNOTO MOKKOKAN
b. Matsumoto-shi, Nagano
c. Matsumoto Mokkodanchi Jigyokyodo Kumiai
d. GK Sekkei Associates ; Takeshi Nishizawa, Noriyuki Asakura
e. Kazuyoshi Watari, Kenji Tamura, Koichi Iwasaki
f. Kitano Construction Corporation
g. Gan Tame
h. A display facilities for DIY (Do It Yourself) training sponsored by the furniture woodworking industry. The facilities are structured of iron and wood, having an expression of an open show case.
i. Japanese larch large cross sectioned laminated lumber / Steel / Cement hollow extruded section panel / Aluminum
j. GK Sekkei Associates

a. 軽井沢高原文庫
b. 長野県軽井沢町
c. 塩沢遊園
d. GK設計　浅倉則幸
e. 渡和由／松永博己
f. 北野建設
g. 岩為
h. 高原の風光と斜面を活かした文学資料展示館，地場の
　浅間石の基壇上に軽快な鉄のシェルターが乗る.
i. コンクリート／スチール／浅間石／ガラス
j. GK設計

a. THE LITERARY MUSEUM OF KARUIZAWA
b. Karuizawa-chyo, Nagano
c. Shiozawa Yuen Co., Ltd.
d. GK Sekkei Associates
e. Kazuyoshi Watari, Hiromi Matsunaga
f. Kitano Construction Corporation
g. Gan Tame
h. A literary museum built with the scenery of the plateau
   and slope made full use of. A light iron shelter rides on
   the stylobate made of regional stone of Asama-seki
   (stone).
i. Concrete / Steel / Asama-seki (stone) / Glass
j. GK Sekkei Associates

a. 進和堂島ビル
b. 大阪府大阪市
c. 進和不動産
e. 竹中工務店設計部　林達雄
f. 竹中工務店
g. 大島勝寛

h. 曲線と直線の対比で, 外観の個性を表し, 大理石と白い
　パネルにあたる光により洒落た雰囲気を持たせた.
i. 大理石／アルミ／ステンレス／シルバーメタリックペンキ
　／アクリル／カラー鉄板
j. 竹中工務店

a. SHINWA DOJIMA BUILDING
b. Osaka-shi, Osaka
c. Shinwa Real Estate Co., Ltd.
e. Takenaka Komuten Co., Ltd., Building Design Depart-
　ment, Tatsuo Hayashi
f. Takenaka Komuten Co., Ltd.
g. Katsuhiro Oshima

h. The individuality of the external appearance of the
　building has been expressed by the contrast between
　curved lines and straight lines, while chic atmosphere
　has been provided by the light reflected from the white
　panel made of marble.
i. Marble / Aluminum / Stainless steel / Silver metallic
　paint / Acryl resin / Color coated steel plate
j. Takenaka Komuten Co., Ltd.

a. 霊友会館横須賀
b. 神奈川県横須賀市
c. 霊友会
e. 竹中工務店設計部　臼井真，菅順二
f. 竹中工務店
g. SS 東京＝大久保公一
h. 端正な外観と集いを誘う外構に依り，心地好い緊張感と
　憩いの中に心のふれあいの場を創出した．
i. 磁器質モザイクタイル／アルミ／ミラーガラス／PC 版アク
　リル系クリアー塗装
j. 竹中工務店

a. YOKOSUKA REIYUKAI COMMUNITY CENTER
b. Yokosuka-shi, Kanagawa
c. The Reiyukai
e. Takenaka Komuten Co., Ltd., Building Design Department　Makoto Usui, Junji Suga
f. Takenaka Komuten Co., Ltd.
g. SS Tokyo Koichi Okubo
h. The classical features of the external appearance and the external structure that invites gathering have created a place where one can hold communion with each other in the atmosphere of pleasant strain and repose.

i. Porcelain mosaic tile / Aluminum / Mirror glass / Acryl resin clear painted PC plate
j. Takenaka Komuten Co., Ltd.

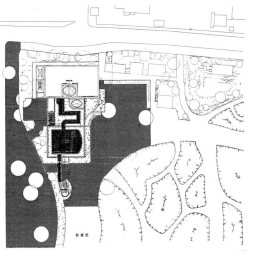

a. 神代植物公園植物会館
b. 東京都調布市
c. 東京都
d. 秀島雅晴／青葉忠之
e. 青葉忠之／加瀬俊一
f. 林建設／富士興業／大気冷熱工業／三菱電気
g. 林建設
h. テーマ＝都市あるいは，地域の"緑の森の中の館"。外部空間と内部空間の融和と拒絶。
i. 炉器質二丁掛タイル（割肌）／花崗岩（桜雲石）／耐候性鋼材／熱線吸収ガラス etc
j. 環境設計研究室

a. THE BOTANICAL CENTER OF JINDAI BOTANI-
   CAL GARDEN
b. Chōfu-shi, Tōkyō
c. Tokyo-to
d. Masaharu Hideshima & Tadayuki Aoba
e. Tadayuki Aoba, Shunichi Kase
f. Construction work : Hayashikensetsu Co., Ltd. ; Electric
   work : Fujikogyo Co., Ltd. ; Mechanical work : Taikir-
   einetsukogyo Co., Ltd.
g. Hayashikensetsu Co., Ltd.
h. The theme of the design is a castle in a city or in a
   regional green wood. Reconciliation and refusal
   between the external space and the internal space.
i. Porcelain double size tile (surface cracked) / Granite /
   Weather resistant steel material / Heat ray absorbing
   glass
j. Environmental Engineering Consultants Co., Ltd.

a. 風のアトリエ
b. 山梨県南都留郡河口湖町
c. 風工学研究所
d. 吉田正昭
e. 矢内定行 (L.A.U.都市施設研究所)／彫刻＝虎竹秀芳
f. 鹿島建設
g. 中田和良
h. 風環境全般の調査・研究を行う我国唯一の民間研究所
　で，日本一の風洞と最新の設備を有する。
i. 富士火山岩／赤御影石／アルミ鋳物 etc
j. L.A.U.都市施設研究所

a. ATELIER WIND
b. Kawaguchiko-chyo, Minamitsuru-gun, Yamanashi
c. Wind's Engineering Institue Co.
d. Masaaki Yoshida
e. Sadayuki Yanai Landscape Architecture, Architechture,
   Urban Planning　Sculpture : Hideyoshi Toratake
f. Kajima Corporation
g. Kazuyoshi Nakada
h. The only private laboratory in Japan where general
   researches and investigations on wind environment are
   conducted, being equipped with the largest wind tunnel
   and latest equipment in Japan.
i. Effusive rock from Mt. Fuji / Red granite / Aluminum
   castings
j. LAU Urban Installation Research Institute

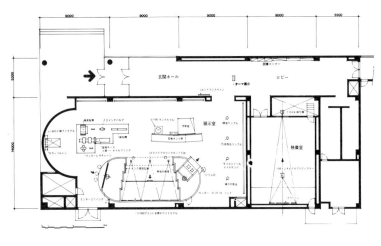

a. サッポロビール開拓使麦酒記念館
b. 北海道札幌市
c. サッポロビール
e. 竹井俊介
f. 大成建設
g. 大成建設
h. 煉瓦造の独特な様式を持つ建物の素朴な架構を十分に引き出し、保存と再生という主題に答えた。
i. レンガ／木材／ステンドグラス／シックイ石／鉄骨
j. 大成建設設計本部

a. THE MEMORIAL HALL OF SAPPORO BREWRIES LIMITED
b. Sapporo-shi, Hokkaido
c. Sapporo Breweries Ltd.
e. Shunsuke Takei
f. Taisei Corporation
g. Taisei Corporation
h. The design has fully responded to the theme of preservation and rehabilitation by bringing out the simple framework from the building of brick in a unique style.
i. Stone / Steel frame
j. Taisei Corporation

a. 福井石油備蓄基地資料館
b. 福井県坂井郡
c. 福井石油備蓄
d. 稲垣博
e. 鈴木恵千代／グラフィックデザイナー＝原田豊，川田憲一／プロモーター＝若林茂樹，山城浩二／プロジェクトマネージャー＝関根謙一／エージェンシー＝電通
f. 乃村工藝社
g. 大東正巳
h. 実物の持つスケール感を十分に表現できる空間構成と、新しいスライド演出手法による展示。
i. 床＝タイルカーペット／壁＝クロス貼／什器＝スチールH型鋼，スチールメラ焼
j. 乃村工藝社

a. MUSEUM OF FUKUI OIL STORAGE BASE
b. Sakai-gun, Fukui
c. Fukui Oil Storage Company Limited
d. Hiroshi Inagaki
e. Shigechiyo Suzuki, Yutaka Harada, Kenichi Kawada, Shigeki Wakabayashi, Koji Yamashiro, Kenichi Sekine, Dentsu Incorporated
f. Nomura Display Co., Ltd.
g. Masami Daito
h. The space is so constructed that the feeling of the scale of the actual equipment can fully be expressed and display can be made by a new representation technique of slide projection.
i. Floor : Tile carpet ; Wall : Cloth covering ; Furniture : Steel H shape section / Melamine resin baking on steel
j. Nomura Display Co., Ltd.

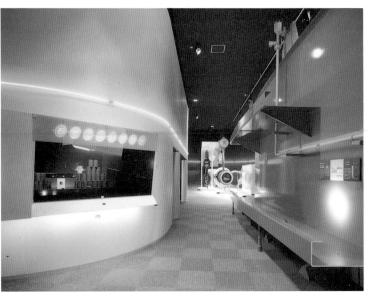

a. 銭湯背景画展「ザ・ニューヨーク, にゅうよく」
b. 東京都渋谷区
c. スクープ
d. 企画構成＝ヨコタデザインワークスタジオ　渡部隆／アートディレクター＝ヨコタデザインワークスタジオ　横田良一
e. 背景画＝背景廣告社　丸山喜久男／グラフィックデザイナー＝矢野豊比古／照明＝クラフト　河合雅樹／音楽＝かしぶち哲郎
f. ゼニヤ
g. 仲佐写真事務所
h. 銭湯の環境としての背景画は決してノスタルジックなモノではなく現代のポップアートを越える面白さを持っている。会場にはコンテンポラリーな銭湯現実空間を構成しビジュアル・音楽・照明を組み合わせながらコミュニケーションの場としての銭湯のあり方を提案し、その空間性をインスタレーションとしてつくりだしているのが今回のエクシビションへの考え方である。
j. ヨコタデザインワークスタジオ

a. SENTO HAIKEIGA-TEN THE NEW YORK, NYUYOKU
b. Shibuya-ku, Tokyo
c. Scoop Inc.
d. Yokota Design Work Stuio Inc. : Ryu Watanabe ; Yokota Design Work Stuio Inc. : Ryoichi Yokota
e. Haikei Kokokusha : Kekuo Maruyama ; Toyohiko Yano ; Kraft : Masaki Kawai ; Tetsuro Kashibuchi
f. Zeniya Co., Ltd.
g. T-Nacasa & Parters
h. The scene painting as an environment of public baths is no way nostalgic but has an interesting aspect exceeding that of contemporary pop art. The concept for the exhibition this time is an attempt to construct an actual space for a contemporary public bath, and to create the nature of the space as an installation by suggesting what a public bath should be as a communication place as combining visuality, music, and lighting.
j. Yokota Design Work Studio Co., Ltd.

a. 青森県観光物産館
b. 青森県青森市
c. 青森県産業振興協会
d. 総括ディレクター=堀田勝之, プランニングディレクター=大野昭夫, 高橋成忠/プランナー=服部実/ディレクター=後藤治/グラフィックディレクター=原田豊/テクニカルディレクター=梅沢誠一郎
e. デザイナー=久光重夫, 川井広光/グラフィックデザイナー=山崎勝巳, 出利葉学/テクニカルデザイナー=宮地克昌/プロモーター=黒石隆夫, 高山敦, 細田豊, 相賀彰, 生駒薫, 野沢紘治
f. 乃村工藝社
g. 大東正巳
h. 産業振興・観光開発の拠点として計画され, 飲食・展示・販売の三つのゾーンて構成されている.
i. ヒバ集整材/合板ラッカー/F.R.P.成型/スチール加工
j. 乃村工藝社

a. AOMORI TOURISM AND PRODUCTS CENTER
b. Aomori-shi, Aomori
c. Aomori Industry Promotion Association
d. Katsuyuki Hotta, Akio Ono, Shigetada Takahashi Minoru Hattori, Osamu Goto, Yutaka Harada, Seiichiro Umezawa
e. Shigeo Hisamitsu, Hiromitsu Kawai, Katsumi Yamazaki, Manabu Ideriha, Katsumasa Miyachi, Takao Kuroishi, Atsushi Takayama, Yutaka Hosoda, Akira Oga, Kaoru Ikoma, Koji Nozawa
f. Nomura Display Co., Ltd.
g. Masami Daito
h. The establishment of this center was planned to set up a strong point for promotion of industry and for development of tourist industry. The center comprises three zones, i.e., eating and drinking, display, and selling.
i. Hiba laminated lumber / Lacquer on plywood / Formed FRP / Steel work
j. Nomura Display Co., Ltd.

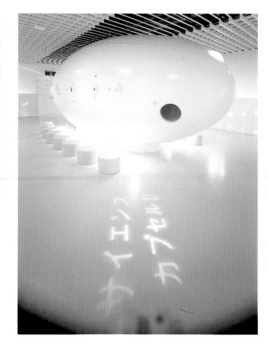

a. 内藤記念くすり博物館
b. 岐阜県羽島郡
c. エーザイ
d. 松村潤之介／プランナー＝鈴木七々夫
e. デザイナー＝鈴木恵千代／グラフィックデザイナー＝原田
　豊，増田雄彦／プロモーター＝福島恵司，森田敬三／
　イラストレーター＝細野修一／コーディネーター＝青木允
　夫／プロジェクトマネージャー＝武居清
f. 乃村工藝社
g. 大東正巳
h. 展示品の保存を最優先に考え，プレーンな平面計画とス
　ケール感のある壁面ケースによる展示．
i. 床＝タイルカーペット／壁＝クロス貼／什器＝タモ柾目染
　色塗装仕上
j. 乃村工藝社

a. THE NAITO MUSEUM OF PHARMACEUTICAL
　SCIENCE AND INDUSTRY
b. Hashima-gun, Gifu
c. Eisai Co., Ltd.
d. Junnosuke Matsumura, Nanao Suzuki
e. Shigechiyo Suzuki, Yutaka Harada, Takahiko Masuda,
　Keiji Fukushima, Keizo Morita, Shuichi Hosono, Mitsuo
　Aoki, Kiyoshi Takei
f. Nomura Display Co., Ltd.
g. Masami Daito
h. Giving priority to the preservation of the exhibits, the
　concept attempted to display them on a plane level and
　in wall cases which affords a large scale feeling.
i. Floor : Tile carpet ; Wall : Cloth covering ; Furniture :
　Color paint finish on tamo straight grain
j. Nomura Display Co., Ltd.

a. 瀧波硝子小さな博物館
b. 東京都墨田区
c. 瀧波硝子
d. 西沢健
e. 設計者＝南和正，藤田雅俊
f. 松屋
g. 上田宏（新建築社）
h. これは墨田区の産業振興キャンペーンとして計画した壁
　の変化により動きと陰影の演出を計った．
i. ボンデ鋼板焼付塗装
j. GK 設計

a. TAKINAMI MINI MUSEUM
b. Sumida-ku, Tokyo
c. Takinami Glass Factory
d. Takashi Nishizawa
e. Kazumasa Minami, Masatoshi Fujita
f. Matsuya
g. Hiroshi Ueda (Shinkenchiku-sha)
h. This museum building was planned with the view of the
　campaign for the promotion of the industry develop-
　ment of Sumida-ku. The concept is an attempt to
　provide movement and shadow through offering a vari-
　ety to the appearance of the wall.
i. Baking paint on bonderized steel sheet
j. GK Sekkei Associates

a. IN'DEX 京都ナショナルショールーム
b. 京都府京都市
c. 松下電器産業
d. 藤岡美和／延藤喜大
e. 小熊幹雄／高山勝己／山下博志／櫃田玲児／飯田良夫／グラフィックデザイナー＝木村正二
f. 千伝社
g. 日本グラフィック
h. ヤングを対象にしたスペース作りで参加性，変化性のあるフレキシブル空間 "百日図鑑" を展開．
i. モルタル／鉄筋CL仕上／H鋼CL仕上／シオジ染色CL／スチールクロウ仕上
j. 千伝社

a. INDEX KYOTO NATIONAL SHOWROOM
b. Kyoto-shi, Kyoto
c. Matsushita Electric Industrial
d. Yoshikazu Fujioka, Yolshihiro Endo
e. Mikio Koguma, Katsumi Takayama, Hiroshi Yamashita, Reiji Hitsuda, Yoshio Iida ; Graphic designer : Shoji Kimura
f. Sendensha Display Co., Ltd.
g. Nippon Graphic
h. Creation of a space intended for the young which invites their participation and is flexible in giving variety, developing a "one hundred day picture book".
i. Cement / CL finish on reinforced concrete / CL finish on H-shape steel / Dye in grain CL finish on Shioji (wood) / Steel chrome prated
j. Sendensha Display Co., Ltd.

a. 竹田製菓「お菓子の城」
b. 愛知県犬山市
c. 竹田製菓
e. 高橋浩
f. 大成建設
g. センターフォト
h. 菓子工場の見学者用施設である．外観は甘いロマンス
　を連想させる中世の小宮殿風白亜の館．
j. 大成建設設計本部

a. THE SWEET CASTLE
b. Inuyama-shi, Aichi
c. Takeda Confetionery Co., Ltd.
e. Hiroshi Takahashi
f. Taisei Corporation
g. Center Photo
h. This building, being the facilities for visitors at a confectionary shop, is a white castle of a type of little palace in the middle age the external appearance of which is associated with sweet romance.
j. Taisei Corporation

a. 東海大学海洋科学博物館マリンサイエンスホール
b. 静岡県清水市
c. 東海大学
d. ディレクター=堀田勝之／プランナー=若月憲夫
e. デザイナー=眞銅将稔，城島敏明／テクニカルデザイナー=中村章，秦直樹／グラフィックデザイナー=川手宏行，金子務，磯川治義／プロモーター=木戸康人，相賀彰，細田豊／マネージャー=武居清
f. 東海教育産業／乃村工藝社
g. 大東正巳
h. 海洋研究情報の発信スペースであり，情報変換に対するシステムを設計コンセプトとしている．
i. ステンレス／合板ラッカー／リノリウム／ビニールクロス
j. 乃村工藝社

a. MARINE SCIENCE MUSEUM TOKAI UNIVERSITY
b. Shimizu-shi, Shizuoka
c. Tokai University
d. Katsuyuki Hotta, Norio Wakatsuki
e. Masatoshi Shindo, Toshiaki Jojima, Akira Nakamura, Naoki Hata, Hiroyuki Kawade, Tsutomu Kaneko, Haruyoshi Isokawa, Yasuto Kido, Akira Oga, Yutaka Hosoda, Kiyoshi Takei
f. Tokai Education ; Nomura Display Co., Ltd. ; Instruments Co., Ltd.
g. Masami Daito
h. This museum is a dispatching space of marine research information. The design concept is an attempt to create a system of information conversion.
i. Stainless steel / Lacquer on plywood / linoleum / Vinyl cloth
j. Nomura Display Co., Ltd.

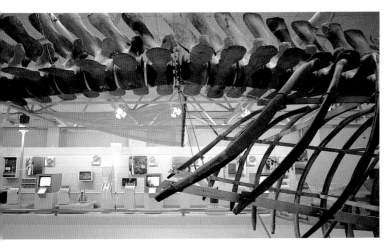

a. 日産ギャラリー JOY JOY 21
b. 埼玉県川口市
c. 日産自動車
d. ジャパンアートプランニングセンター　玉置朝男
e. 玉置朝男　ジャパンアートプランニングセンター／マネージメント＝商工美術　田中和行／プロデュース＝日放野口健
f. 商工美術
g. 大東正巳
h. 複数のメーカーの総合ショールーム内の NISSAN ブース.
i. 床＝ナラフローリング，ゴムタイル貼り／壁＝VP吹付，6面ビジョン入り
j. ジャパンアートプランニングセンター

a. NISSAN GALLERY JOY JOY 21
b. Kawaguchi-shi, Saitama
c. Nissan
d. Japan Art Planning Center Co., Ltd.
e. Japan Art Planning Center Co., Ltd. : Asao Tamaki / Shoko Bijutsu : Kazuyuki Tanaka / Nippo : Ken Noguchi
f. Shoko Bijutsu
g. Masami Daito
h. Nissan booth in the comprehensive show room of makers.
i. Floor : Japanese oak wood flooring / Rubber tile flooring ; Wall : VP spraying / Visions on 6-surfaces
j. Japan Art Planning Center Co., Ltd.

a. マツダロータリー御堂筋
b. 大阪府大阪市
c. マツダ
d. アートディレクター＝田中一光／ディレクター＝秋山茂樹
e. 柳川光雄／坪坂博文／川勝英史／花岡豊／プロモーター＝山崎尚人
f. 乃村工藝社
h. "パブリック"を意図した全体構成，多目的に展開されるイベント用の自走マルチビデオ，ツール群．
i. 単層フローリング／御影石／メラミン焼付け鋼板／岩綿吸音板／スチールメッシュ
j. 乃村工藝社

a. MAZDA ROTARY MIDOSUJI
b. Osaka-shi, Osaka
c. Mazda Motor Corporation
d. Ikko Tanaka
e. Mitsuo Yanagawa, Hirofumi Tsubosaka, Hidefumi Kawa-katsu, Yutaka Hanaoka, Naoto Yamazaki
f. Nomura Display Co., Ltd.
h. The whole construction is an attempt at seeking "publicity". A mobile multi-video set for showing events that are developed for multipurpose use, and other various kinds of tools.
i. Single layer flooring / Granite / Melamine baking on steel plate / Asbestos sound absorbing board / Steel mesh
j. Nomura Display Co., Ltd.

a. 富士通プラザ・OBP
b. 大阪府大阪市
c. 富士通
d. 博報堂／ウィーズ・ブレーン／GK設計
e. GK設計
f. 熊谷組／製作＝丹青社
g. 仲佐写真事務所
h. 可変する大道具・小道具により様々な展示機能に対応する舞台としてのショウルームを実現した．
i. 天然木化粧シート／スチール／大理石／ガラスノフリーアクセスフロア
j. GK設計

a. FUJITSU PLAZA OBP
b. Osaka-shi, Osaka
c. Fujitsu Limited
d. Hakuhodo Incorporated ; We's Brain ; GK Sekkei Associates
e. GK Sekkei Associates
f. Kumagai Gumi Co., Ltd. ; Tanseisha Co., Ltd.
g. Nacasa Ph Partners
h. A show room has been realized as a stage which accommodates a variety of displaying functions by the help of variable stage settings and stage properties.
i. Natural wood veneered sheet / Steel / Marble / Glass / Free access floor
j. GK Sekkei Associates

a. 仙台第一生命タワービルディング
b. 宮城県仙台市
c. 第一生命保険
e. 竹中工務店設計部　榎本和夫，有角昇純，広島正明
f. 竹中工務店／日本建設共同企業体
g. 村井修
h. 眺望を重視したゆとりある共用空間の提供，並びに，緑
　豊かな環境に調和した建物とする.
i. カナダ産花崗岩／イタリア産大理石／アルミ／ガラス／
　樹木 (桂／ベンジャミン)
j. 竹中工務店

a. SENDAI DAI-ICHI SEIMEI TOWER BUILDING
b. Sendai-shi, Miyagi
c. The Dai-ichi Mutual life Insurance Company
e. Takenaka Komuten Co., Ltd, Building Design Department. Kazuo Enomoto, Noriyoshi Arikado, Masaaki
   Hiroshima
f. Takenaka Komuten Co., Ltd. ; Nihon Kensetsu Joint
   Venture
g. Osamu Murai
h. The presentation of a common space that allows much
   latitude with special emphasis on a nice view, and a
   building that well matches the environment rich in
   green.
i. Granite from Canada / Marble from Italy / Aluminum /
   Glass / Wood (Katsura tree / Benjamin tree)
j. Takenaka Komuten Co., Ltd.

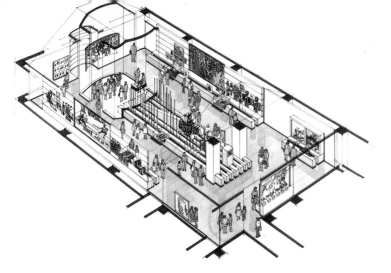

a. 豊田市棒の手会館
b. 愛知県豊田市
c. 豊田市
d. アートディレクター＝平林寛史
e. 平林寛史／石塚直子
f. 乃村工藝社
g. パープランニング
h. 猿投祭りは、献馬と棒の手奉納の祭りである。献馬を中央にして行列を組み行進している様子を物中心にした大ステージで展開し、映像により祭りの興奮を再現している。
i. ステージ＝タモ材染色加工・演示メッシュパネル／演示パネル＝タモ材染色加工・クロス貼り
j. 乃村工藝社

a. BOHNOTE MUSEUM OF TOYOTA
b. Toyota-shi, Aichi
c. Toyota City
d. Hirofumi Hirabayashi
e. Hirofumi Hirabayashi, Naoko Ishizuka
f. Nomura Display Co., Ltd.
g. Par Planning
h. "Sarunage-matsuri" is a festival for dedicating a house and "Bonnote". The actions of a parade marching with a dedicated horse in the middle has been developed on a large stage, and the excitement of the festival has been reproduced by the help of video (or screen image).
i. Stage : Dye in grain on tamo wood / Presentation mesh panel ; Presentation mesh panel : Dye in grain on tamo wood / cloth covering
j. Nomura Display Co., Ltd.

a. 仙台市博物館
b. 宮城県仙台市
c. 仙台市
d. アートディレクター＝髙野祐之
e. 藤崎治郎／平林寛史／プロデュース＝山田昌之
f. 乃村工藝社
g. 大東正巳
h. 当博物館を構成する各展示室は、独自のファサードをもっている。都市空間の隠諭によるデザイン。
i. 床＝ナラフローリング、カーペット他／壁＝プラスター、石貼他
j. 乃村工藝社

a. SENDAI CITY MUSEUM
b. Sendai-shi, Miyagi
c. Sendai City
d. Yasuyuki Takano
e. Jiro Fujisaki, Hirofumi Hirabayashi, Masayuki Yamada
f. Nomura Display Co., Ltd.
g. Masami Daito
h. Each show room constituting this museum has its own unique facade. The design relates to the metaphor of an urban space.
i. Floor : Japanese oak flooring / Carpet ; Wall : Plaster / Stone Paneling
j. Nomura Display Co., Ltd.

a. 日産自動車追浜工場PR会館
b. 神奈川県横須賀市
c. 日産自動車
d. ジャパンアートプランニングセンター　玉置朝男
e. ジャパンアートプランニングセンター　玉置朝男／アシスタントデザイナー＝前田和彦／マネージメント＝商工美術　田中和行
f. 商工美術　福山高志
g. 大東正巳
h. 既存建物内に小学生を対象とした自動車のPR会館を設置。コンセプトワークからユーザーまでを表現。
i. スチールメラ焼付／透明ガラス／スリガラスフッソ処理／ワイヤー吊り
j. ジャパンアートプランニングセンター

a. NISSAN OPPAMA PR CENTER
b. Yokosuka-shi, Kanagawa
c. Nissan
d. Japan Art Planning Center Co., Ltd. : Asao Tamaki
e. Japan Art Planning Center Co., Ltd. : Asao Tamaki, Kazuhiko Maeda / Shoko Bijutsu : Kazuyuki Tanaka
f. Shoko Bijutsu : Takashi Fukuyama
g. Masami Daito
h. A school-children-oriented PR Center of automobiles has been installed, where full particulars from the conceptual work to user-related matters have been expressed.
i. Melamine baking on steel / Transparent glass / Ground glass / fluorine treated / wiring suspension
j. Japan Art Planning Center Co., Ltd.

a. パナソニック・スクェア
b. 大阪府大阪市
c. 松下電器産業
d. 栗原稔
e. 田村真一／田村恭男
f. 乃村工藝社
h. 商品は直接前面に出さず、楽しく参加しながら理解してもらう、新しいスタイルのショールーム.
j. 乃村工藝社

a. PANASONIC SQUARE
b. Osaka-shi, Osaka
c. Matsushita Electric Industrial Co., Ltd.
d. Minoru Kurihara
e. Shinichi Tamura, Yasuo Tamura
f. Nomura Display Co., Ltd.
h. A new style of show room where articles do not appear to be directly put forward before the visitors but are so laid out that the visitors can understand the article as being invited to participate pleasantly.
j. Nomura Display Co., Ltd.

a. KAKURI ディスプレイブース
b. 東京都中央区
c. 角利産業
d. 刈屋剛
e. 刈屋剛
f. 商工宣伝社
g. 刈屋剛
h. '86年第9回日本DIYショー出展.
j. アスカデザイン室

a. KAKURI CO. BOOTH
b. Chuo-ku, Tokyo
c. Kakuri Corporation
d. GO Kariya
e. GO Kariya
f. Shoko Ad. Inc.
g. GO Kariya
h. This booth is for exhibition in the Ninth Japan DIY Show 1986.
j. Aska Inc.

a. O.B.P.ギャラリーツイン21
b. 大阪府大阪市
c. 松下興産ツインタワー
d. 小林進／村田公昭／郷力憲治
e. 前田穂積／上野政彦／三嶽伊紗／八幡はるみ／松尾恵／大崎信之
f. 西武百貨店関西／乃村工藝社
g. 村瀬武男
h. 地・水・火・風をテーマにそれぞれ金属・石・木・紙の自然素材により，造形的な構成を試みた。
i. 砂岩／スプルス／うるし／和紙／サビ鉄／真鍮／スチール
j. 乃村工藝社

a. O.B.P. GALLERY TWIN 21
b. Osaka-shi, Osaka
c. MID Twin Tower
d. Susumu Kobayashi, Kimiaki Murata, Kenji Goriki
e. Hozumi Maeda, Masahiko Ueno, Isa Mitake, Harumi Yarumi, Megumi Matsuo, Nobuyuki Osaki
f. Nomura Display Co., Ltd.
g. Takeo Murase
h. The concept is an attempt at creating a formative composition, with ground, water, fire, and wind as a theme, by using natural materials of metal, stone, wood, and paper.
i. Sand rock / Spruce / Lacquer / Japanese paper / Stained iron / Brass / Steel
j. Nomura Display Co., Ltd.

a. 竹原火力展示館
b. 広島県竹原市
c. 電源開発
d. 津田雅人
e. 平林寛史
f. 乃村工藝社
g. 大東正己
h. 「竹原火力展示館」ではメディア表現の革新をめざし、単一の空間が重層的な情報発進機能を持つこと、さらに人間と人間の対話性を充足する場の創造を展開の基本理念とした。また、環境構成的な体験映像が中心となって、時空間を自在に変容させつつ力強い生命を帯びながら人々の"知と感"に向けてビジュアルなメッセージを放射するよう計画した。
i. ステージ＝タモ染色加工／グラフィックパネル＝フロートガラス・スリ板加工／装置模型＝樹脂加工
j. 乃村工藝社

a. EXHIBITION HALL TAKEHARA THERMAL POWER STATION
b. Takehara-shi, Hiroshima
c. Electric Power Development Co., Ltd.
d. Masato Tsuda
e. Hirofumi Hirabayashi
f. Nomura Display Co., Ltd.
g. Masami Daito
h. In constructing the "Exhibition Hall TAKEHARA Thermal Power station", the basic concept, aiming at the renovation of media expression, is an attempt to create a place where even a single space can have diversified information-sending functions, and will moreover satisfy the easiness of dialogue between human beings. The scheme attempts to allow the space to project visual messages that are centered around the reflection of the experience of environmental structure toward the senses of justice of people by way of metamorphosing at will the space time with powerful life inspired.
i. Stage : Dye in grain finishing on tamo (Wood) ; Graphic panel : Float glass grinding ; Equipment model : Resin works
j. Nomura Display Co., Ltd.

a. CITY POLE
b. 大阪府大阪市
c. 大光
e. 池上俊郎／池上明
f. 間組大阪支店
g. GRAIN＝宗田晶
h. 都市中心部の狭小敷地、意図的斜線、3種5色の素材、形態的奥行により、都市の原点を構成。
i. 外壁＝ネオパリエ、アルミパネル（t=2.0）、二丁掛タイル、RC打放し／アプローチ＝二丁掛タイル
j. アーバンガウス研九所

a. CITY POLE
b. Osaka-shi, Osaka
c. Daiko Inc.
e. Toshiro Ikegami, Akira Ikegami
f. Hazama-gumi Ltd., Osaka-shiten
g. Grain : Akira Shoda
h. A narrow site in the heart of the city. The original point of the city has been structured by the use of intentional oblique lines, three kinds of five colors, and morphological depth.
i. Wall : Neopalie (artificial marble) / Aluminum panel (t= 0.2) ; Double size tile / Fair-faced concrete ; Approach : Double size tile
j. Urbangauss

a. 的野歯科医院
b. 福岡県福岡市
c. 的野良次
e. 竹中工務店設計部　奥嶋寛治／波多江繁
f. 竹中工務店
g. 岡本公二
h. ボックスアーキテクチャーを原形。パーゴラや曲面の壁を採用しシャープで清潔感ある建物を企図。
i. 吹付タイル／アルミ／ガラス
j. 竹中工務店

a. MATONO DENTAL CLINIC
b. Fukuoka-shi, Fukuoka
c. Ryozi Matono
e. Takenaka Komuten Co., Ltd. Building Design Department ; Kanji Okushima, Shigeru Hatae
f. Takenaka Komuten Co., Ltd.
g. Koji Okamoto
h. Box architecture is an original form of this design. The scheme attempts to create a building that is sharp as well as has the sense of cleanliness by the adoption of a pergola and curved-surface walls.
i. Spray-on tile / Aluminum / Glass
j. Takenaka Komuten Co., Ltd.

a. D・A・N・T・O　SHOWROOM
b. 北海道札幌市
c. 淡陶
e. SEMBA 設計事務所　ちばまさゆき
f. 船場札幌営業所
g. 安達治
h. 銀ネズ色・桜桃・藤紫・緋色・色・散・華・江戸の夜ここは遊びの別天地現世の結果，格子の天女の艶くらべ……．
i. 床＝カーペット貼／天井＝EP 塗装／壁面＝EP 塗装／什器＝ラッカー塗装
j. SEMBA 設計事務所札幌

a. D.A.N.T.O SHOWROOM
b. Sapporo-shi, Hokkaido
c. Danto Co., Ltd.
e. Masayuki Chiba
f. Semba Sapporo Eigyosho
g. Osamu Adachi
h. Silver gray, pink, dark lilac, scarlet, and other colors ; Buddhist rite of scattering flowers ; a night in Edo ; this place here is another planet of play ; the outcome of the this life ; the contest of charmingness of heavenly maidens sitting behind the latticework.
i. Floor : Carpet laying ; Ceiling : EP painting ; Wall : EP painting ; Furniture : Lacquer painting
j. Semba Corporation

a. 皆川クリニック・ビル
b. 大阪府大東市
c. 皆川
d. 清川卓史
e. 野口峰三郎／石橋信男
f. 淀建設工業
g. 大東フォート (溝口宏)
h. "野崎参り"で有名な商店街の真中に建つ総合医療ビル……。街の景観に素直に馴じむデザイン。
i. ALC ／タイル／色ガラス／ガラスブロック
j. 富士建築設計事務所

a. MINAGAWA CLINIC
b. Daito-shi, Osaka
c. Minagawa Co., Ltd.
d. Takafumi Kiyokawa
e. Minesaburo Noguchi, Nobuo Ishibashi
f. Yodo General Construction Co., Ltd.
g. Daito Photo (Hiroshi Mizoguchi)
h. The comprehensive medical building standing in the center of the shopping mall famous for "Nozaki visiting". The design is such that the architecture is easily integrated into the landscape of the mall.
i. ALC / Tile / Colored glass / Glass block
j. Fuji Architect Corporation

a. レリーフ「大樹」
b. 香川県善通寺市
c. 善通寺市
e. 萩原克彦設計事務所　協力=時忠彦（プラスデザインオフィス）
f. ナスエンジニアリング
g. 新建築社写真部
h. 公共建築の吹抜壁面のレリーフ．テーマは"市の木"「楠」．
i. ステンレス製（鏡面仕上げ）
j. 萩原克彦設計事務所

a. RELIEF "TAIJU" (BIG TREE)
b. Zentsuji-shi, Kagawa
c. Zentsuji-shi
e. Katsuhiko Hagiwara Architect & Associates Associate : Tadahiko Toki (Plas Design Office)
f. Nas Engineering Co., Ltd.
g. The Japan Architect Co., Ltd.
h. A relief on the wall surface of the stair well in a public building. The theme is the city tree, "camphor tree".
i. Stainless steel make (mirror finish)
j. Katsuhiko Hagiwara Architect & Associates

4.商業・レジャー環境デザイン

店舗
複合商業施設
ショッピングモール
百貨店
ホテル
スポーツ施設
レジャーランド
これらの外構および造園デザイン
etc.

4. Commercial and Leisure Environmental Design

Stores
Commercial complexes
Shopping Malls
Acades
Hotels
Sports facilities
Recreational facilities and other related outdoor design
etc.

a. つかしんヤングライブ館
b. 兵庫県尼崎市
c. 西武百貨店関西
d. シティクリエイト　水尾和明／西武百貨店販売促進部
　 岡本紘治郎
e. 月足周平／角田辰之／岡田小百合
f. 西武百貨店建装部
g. フォトスG　後藤保弘
h. 複合商業施設「つかしん」専門店ゾーンの核店舗として
　 ヤングの五感に訴える30店舗の集積.
i. 共通部分:床=別注レンガタイル+枕木／壁面=PB 貼
　 EP 塗装／天井=一部スティールルーバー
j. アルス大阪店

a. TSUKASHIN YOUNG LIVE KAN
b. Amagasaki-shi, Hyogo
c. The Seibu Department Stores Kansai
d. City Create Ltd.: Kazuaki Mizuo ; The Seibu Depart-
　 ment Stores : Kojiro Okamoto
e. Shuhei Tsukiashi, Tatsuyuki Sumida, Sayuri Okada
f. The Seibu Department Stores
g. Photos-G Yasuhiro Goto
h. A commercial complex "Tsukashin" -an integration of
　 30 shops that, as the nuclear shop group in the special-
　 ity shop zone, appeals to the sense of the young.
i. Common part : Order-made brick tile+sleeper ; Wall :
　 EP coating on PB lining ; Ceiling : Partly steel louver
j. Arusu Co., Ltd.

a. 生活遊園地「つかしん」
b. 兵庫県尼崎市
c. 西武百貨店関西
d. プロデューサー＝西洋環境開発／西武百貨店／アート
　ディレクター＝魚成祥一郎，関口敏美，大菅史郎
e. 久保茂，森隆城，木屋久男，藤本強，蔭山力雄，宮
　下淳，北川英康，柳川敏行，中野誠一／アーティスト＝
　河合隆三，木田安彦，環境デザイン研究所
f. SPN／乃村工藝社
g. 村瀬武男／柴谷浩也
j. 乃村工藝社商業施設開発事業部

a. TSUKASHIN
b. Amagasaki, Hyogo
c. The Seibu Department Stores Kansai
d. Producer : Seiyo Environment Development ; The Seibu
Department Stores / Art Director : Shoichiro Uonari,
Toshimi Sekiguchi, Shiro Osuga
e. Shigeru Kubo, Takaki Mori, Hisao Kiya, Tsuyoshi Fujimoto, Rikio Kageyama, Jun Miyashita, Hideyasu Kitagawa, Toshiyuki Yanagawa, Seiichi Nakano / Artist :
Ryuzo Kawai, Yasuhiko Kida ; Environment Design Institute

f. S.P.N Co., Ltd. ; Nomura Display Co., Ltd.
g. Takeo Murase, Hiroya Shibatani
i. Nomura Display Co., Ltd.

a. 生活遊園地「つかしん」
b. 兵庫県尼崎市
c. 西武百貨店関西
d. プロデューサー＝西洋環境開発，西武百貨店／アートディレクター＝魚成祥一郎，関口敏美，大菅史郎
e. 久保茂，森隆城，木屋久男，藤本強，蔭山力雄，宮下淳，北川英康，柳川敏行，中野誠一／アーティスト＝河合隆三，木田安彦，環境デザイン研究所
f. SPN／乃村工藝社
g. 村瀬武男／柴谷浩也
j. 乃村工藝社商業施設開発事業部

a. TSUKASHIN
b. Amagasaki-shi, Hyogo
c. The Seibu Department Stores Kansai
d. Producer : Seibu Environment Development ; The Seibu Department Stores / Art Director : Shoichiro Uonari, Toshimi Sekiguchi, Shiro Osuga
e. Shigeru Kubo, Takaki Mori, Hisao Kiya, Tsuyoshi Fujimoto, Rikio Kageyama, Jun Miyashita, Hideyasu Kitagawa, Toshiyuki Yanagawa, Seiichi Nakano / Artist : Ryuzo Kawai, Yasuhiko Kida ; Environment Design Institute
f. S.P.N Co., Ltd. ; Nomura Display Co., Ltd.
g. Takeo Murase, Hiroya Shibatani
j. Nomura Display Co., Ltd.

a. 丸八真綿東京本部ビル
b. 東京都港区
c. 丸八真綿
e. 鹿島建設建築設計本部／丹青社
f. 鹿島建設
g. 川澄建築写真事務所

h. 120度V型のミラーガラスの万華鏡効果をねらった，寝具の総合ショールーム．
i. ミラーガラス／大型セラミック板（本邦初の試み）
j. 鹿島建設建築設計本部

a. MARUHATI AOYAMA BUILDING
b. Minato-ku, Tokyo
c. Hatchi Co., Ltd.
e. Kajima Corporation, Architectural Design Division / Tansei sha
f. Kajima Corporation
g. Kawasumi Architectural Photograph Office

h. The concept aims at creating a Kaleidoscope effect out of the V-shaped mirror glass at an angle of 120 degrees. A comprehensive bedclothes show room.
i. Mirror glass / Large size ceramic palte (the first trial in Japan)
j. Kajima Corporation

a. 新ゆりグリーンプラザ・シンボルタワー
b. 神奈川県川崎市
c. 日本勤労者住宅協会
e. 萩原克彦設計事務所
f. 鴻池組／ナスエンジニアリング
g. アトム写真
h. ショッピング施設のシンボルとして，また営業中のサインとして電動で回転する。
i. ステンレス（鏡面仕上げ）／ベースは打放しコンクリート／樹脂塗装
j. 萩原克彦設計事務所

a. SIMBOL TOWER OF SHINYURI GREEN PLAZA
b. Kawasaki-shi, Kanagawa
c. Nihon Kinrosha Jutaku Kyokai
e. Katsuhiko Hagiwara Architect & Associates
f. F. Konoike-Gumi, Nas Engineering Co., Ltd.
g. Atom Photo
h. As a symbol of the shopping center and a sign for "Open", the symbol tower rotates by electric power.
i. Made of stainless steel (mirror finish) / Base: Fair faced concrete / Resin painting
j. Katsuhiko Hagiwara Architect & Associates

a. わくわく CITY
b. 大阪府大坂市
c. チェーンストア オークワ
d. 香川英行
e. 基本計画＝水町淳二／安藤一利　建築設計＝I・N・A
　　新建築研究所　相宮常雄, 奥優

f. 村本建設
g. アトリエ・フクモト (福本正明)
j. 船場 SC 綜合開発研究所

a. WAKUWAKU CITY
b. Osaka-shi, Osaka
c. Chain Store Okuwa, Inc.
d. Hideyuki Kagawa
e. Planning : Junji Mizumachi, Kazutoshi Ando / Designer :
　　Institute of New Architecture, Inc. Tsuneo Somiya,
　　Masaru Oku

f. Muramoto Construction
g. Atelier Hukumoto (Masaaki Hukumoto)
j. Semba Corporation

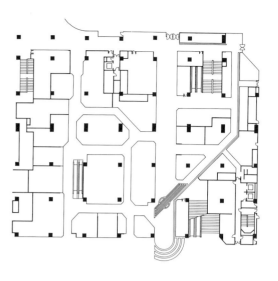

a. なんば CITY "シティレディース・リニューアル"
b. 大阪府大阪市
c. 南海電気鉄道
d. プロデューサー＝岩城章嗣　アートディレクター＝久保茂
e. 木屋久男，角谷修／コーディネーター＝中村勉，山田文夫
f. 乃村工藝社
g. 村瀬武男
j. 乃村工藝社商業施設開発事業部

a. NANBA CITY "CITY LADIES RENEWAL"
b. Osaka-shi, Osaka
c. Nankai Electric Railway
d. Producer : Akitsugu Iwaki / Art director : Shigeru Kubo
e. Hisao Kiya, Osamu Kadoya / Coordinator : Tsutomu Nakamura, Fumio Yamada
f. Nomura Display Co., Ltd.
g. Takeo Murase
j. Nomura Display Co., Ltd.

a. 下田サンプラーザ「Ami」レストラン街
b. 静岡県下田市
c. サンプラーザ
d. 窪本貴司
e. 小薗江龍治
f. 伊豆急ハウジング／河津建設
h.「ウェストコーストの白い風」――昼のスポーツ，夜のドライブの後に立ち寄るカジュアルな空間．
i. サイディングボード／磁器タイル
j. 船場

a. SHIMODA SUN PLAZA "AMI" RESTAURANRTS
b. Shimoda-shi, Shizuoka
c. Inc. Sun Plaza
d. Takashi Kubomoto
e. Ryuji Osonoe
f. Inc., Izukyu Housing, Kawazu Kensetsu Inc.
h. "White wind blowing along the West coast" - A casual space to stop by after sporting in the daytime and driving at night.
i. Siding board
j. Semba Corporation

a. 軽井沢サムタイムハウス
b. 長野県軽井沢町
c. 日本たばこ産業
d. 匹田定嘉（電通映画社）
e. 設計企画＝塚原正一／キャラクター＝高橋新三, 川崎修司／照明＝海藤春樹
f. 小林工芸社
g. 高橋克明
h. 風と太陽をいっぱい取り入れるべくオープンなかたちにこだわり建物自体をサインとした.
i. 鉄骨軸組／角材／合板ベニヤ／塗装仕上
j. 小林工芸社

a. KARUIZAWA SOMETIME HOUSE
b. Karuizawa-machi, Nagano
c. Japan Tobacco Inc.
d. Sadayoshi Hikita
e. Planning : Syoichi Tsukahara / Character : Shinzo Takahashi, Syuji Kawasaki / Lighting : Haruki Kaito
f. Kobayashi Kogeisha Co., Ltd.
g. Katsuaki Takahashi
h. In sticking to the configuration of "open space" so as to fully take in wind and sunlight, the scheme attempted to make the building itself a sign board.
i . Steel frame structure / Square timber / Plywood veneer / Painting finish
j. Kobayashi Kogeisha Co., Ltd.

a. 近鉄百貨店橿原店
b. 奈良県橿原市
c. 近鉄百貨店
d. 近鉄百貨店経営企画室
e. 竹中工務店／乃村工藝社
f. 奥村組，竹中工務店，大林組，大日本土木，村本建設
g. 竹中工務店
h. 古代文化発祥の地に立つ当百貨店は，大和三山等の地域の色・形をデザインモチーフにしている．
i. 外壁＝特殊樹脂型枠コンクリートの上に弾性塗料／内壁＝ネオパリエ　他
j. 竹中工務店

a. THE KASHIHARA KINTETSU DEPARTMENT STORE
b. Kashihara-shi, Nara
c. Kintetsu Department Store Co., Ltd.
d. Management Planning Depart. I.
e. Takenaka Komuten Co., Ltd. / Nomura Display Co., Ltd.
f. Okumura；Takenaka Komuten；Ohbayashi, Dainihon Doboku, Muramoto Construction
g. Takenaka Komuten Co., Ltd.
h. This department store, standing on the cradle of ancient civilization, incorporates into the design motif the colors and configurations of the regional area of Yamato three-bigtemples.
i. External wall：Plastic paint on concrete wall using special resin frame；Internal wall：Artificial marble (Neopalie) and others
j. Takenaka Komuten Co., Ltd.

a. イーストランド
b. 岡山県津山市
c. 三和
d. 神尾勝宏
e. 植山敏朗／竹内幸代／鈴木裕之
f. 大本組
g. 福本正明
h. 建物の内外装にアクセサリーを使うことにより，スペシャルでユニークなSC創りを心がける.
i. 40×70の2Jタイル
j. 船場SC綜合開発研究所

a. EAST-LAND
b. Tsuyama-shi, Okayama
c. Sanwa
d. Katsuhiro Kamio
e. Toshiro Ueyama, Sachiyo Takeuchi, Hiroyuki Suzuki
f. Omoto-Gumi
g. Masaaki Fukumoto
h. The concept is an attempt at creating unique, special SC by using accessories on both interior and exterior of the building.
i. 40×70 double size tile
j. Semba Corporation

a. グリナード永山パブリックスペース
b. 東京都多摩市
c. 新都市センター開発
d. 奥住マネージメント研究所, 田中理夫 (清水建設設計本部デザインセンター)
e. 横沢英一 (彫刻家)／崇島志知郎 (清水建設設計本部デザインセンター)／ランドスケープデザインコンサルタント
f. 清水建設／黒髪石材／横沢彫刻研究所
g. 清水建設
h. 石彫と水の組合せで，手仕事のわざをもって爽やかなくつろぎのインドアレストエリアを提供した.
i. 彫刻＝徳山御影／舗装＝大理石／ファニチャー＝木と鉄
j. 横沢英一

a. GREENADE NAGAYAMA PUBLIC SPACE
b. Tama-shi, Tokyo
c. Shintomi Center Kaihatsu Co., Ltd.
d. Okuzumi Management Research : Masao Tanaka (Shimizu Construction Co., Ltd.)
e. Sculpter : Hidekazu Yokozawa / Shimizu Construction Co., Ltd. : Shichiro Takashima / Landscape Design Consultant
f. Shimizu Construction Co., Ltd. ; Kurokami Sekizai Co., Ltd. ; Yokozawa Sculpter Studio
g. Shimizu Construction Co., Ltd.
h. An indoor rest area has been presented in which refreshing and relaxed feeling is afforded by the help of the combination of curved stones and water and handworkings.
i. Sculpture / Tokuyama granite / Pavement / Marble / Furniture / Wood and iron
j. Hidekazu Yokozawa

a. ジャスコ新茨木店
b. 大阪府茨木市
c. ジャスコ
d. 岡西昭雄／山本忠夫
e. 東本源盛／玉置喜久／池田忠
f. 船場／間組
g. 福本正明
h. "ダイナミック＆グレイシー"をテーマに新鮮でかつ新時代を予感させる高感度空間の創造を目指す.
i. モザイクタイル／ワーロン
j. 船場SC綜合開発研究所

a. JUSCO SHIN IBARAKI
b. Ibaraki-shi, Osaka
c. Jusco
d. Akio Okanishi, Tadao Yamamoto
e. Gensho Tomoto, Tamaki Yoshihisa, Tadashi Ikeda
f. Semba Corporation
g. Masaaki Fukumoto
h. With dynamism and grace as a theme, the concept aims at creating a fresh space sensitive enough to allow people to sense the advent of a new age.
i. Mosaic tile
j. Semba Corporation

a. テーオーシー ROX ビル
b. 東京都台東区
c. テーオーシー
e. 可児才介
f. 大成建設
g. 大成建設
h. 伝統の町浅草に時代の先端をゆくハイテックでヒューマンで何度でも行きたくなる複合商業施設.
i. フッ素樹脂塗装 PC 版／ラスター釉磁器タイル／フッ素樹脂焼付鉄板／アルミサッシ
j. 大成建設設計本部

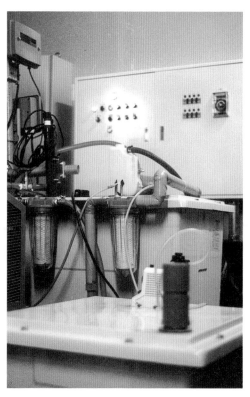

a. T.O.C. ROX
b. Taito-ku, Tokyo
c. T.O.C. Co., Ltd.
e. Saisuke Kani
f. Taisei Corporation
g. Taisei Corporation
h. A commercial complex development which is humane and makes people feel like visiting there many times because of its high technology in the van of the era set in the traditional downtown, Asakusa.
i. Fluorine contained resin painted PC board / Luster glazedporcelain tile / Fluorine-containing-resin baked steel plate / Aluminum sash
j. Taisei Corporation

a. センターフォーラム
b. 宮城県仙台市
c. I・4・I
d. 竹居正武　ダムダン空間工作所
e. 設計企画=鈴木隆行　ダムダン空間工作所／小長井雅昭　アラップインターナショナル
f. アラップインターナショナル
h. 土を使わない室内植栽により清潔さと軽量化を図り、マイコンによる自動管理を可能にした。
i. ロックウールグロダン／ハイドロボール／RISドリップセット
j. アラップインターナショナル

a. CENTER-FORUM
b. Sendai-shi, Miyagi
c. Ichi-Yon-Ichi Corporation
d. Dam-Dan Corporation : Masatake Takei
e. Dam-Dan Corporation : Takayuki Suzuki / ALAP International Inc. : Masaaki Konagai
f. ALAP International Inc.
h. The realization of cleanliness and downsize by the adoption of soilless interior planting has enabled the automatic control by a microcomputer.
i. Rock wool / Hydroball / RIS drip set
j. ALAP International Inc.

a. 茅ヶ崎ルミネ
b. 神奈川県茅ヶ崎市
c. 湘南ステーション開発
d. 峰寛
e. 佐藤治郎
f. アルス
g. アルス
j. アルスHED事業部

a. CHIGASAKI LUMINE
b. Chigasaki-shi, Kanagawa
c. Shyonan Station Development
d. Hiroshi Mine
e. Jiro Sato
f. Arusu Co., Ltd.
g. Arusu Co., Ltd.
j. Arusu Co., Ltd.

a. 加茂ショッピングパークメリア
b. 新潟県加茂市
c. 加茂 SC 協同組合／まるよし
d. 高橋陸三郎
e. 松本一哉／建築設計＝青柳設計・小林設計 JV
f. 清水建設／内装＝船場
h. 駅前の区画整理事業に伴う「まるよし」を核とした地元主
　 導型のショッピングセンター.
i. 磁器質タイル／ALC 板アクリル弾性塗装
j. 船場

a. KAMO SHOPPING PARK MELIA
b. Kamo-shi, Niigata
c. Kamo S.C. Cooperative Associatin Inc. Maruyoshi
d. Rikusaburo Takahashi
e. Kazuya Matsumoto/ Architect : J.V. of Inc. Aoyagi Sek-
　 kei & Inc. Kobayashi Sekkei
f. Shimizu Construction Co., Ltd. ; Semba Corporation
h. A shopping center of a local-end-initiative type that has
　 been developed around the nucleus of "Maruyoshi" in
　 association with the project of the land readjustment of
　 the station front.
i. Procelain tile / ALC plate / Acryl elastic painting
j. Semba Corporation

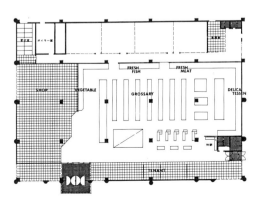

a. サンドール北海道伏古店
b. 北海道札幌市
c. 橋本倉庫
e. SEMBA 設計事務所　ちばまさゆき＋児玉有弘
f. 共立建設・丸竹竹田組 JV
g. 安達治
h. 地域風土感によるデザイン……大地からの愛！
i. 外壁＝打放し，カラー鉄板，銅板，米松丸太半割／床＝テラゾー貼／内装壁＝PB クロス貼
j. SEMBA 設計事務所札幌

a. SUNDORE HOKKAIDO FUSHIKO
b. Sapporo-shi, Hokkaido
c. Hashimoto Sohko
e. Senba Corporation Masayuki Chiba, Arihiro Kodama
f. Kuyoritsu Kensetsu ; Marutake Takeda-Gumi JV
g. Osamu Adachi
h. A design based on the natural features of the region-a love from the earth!
i. External wall : Fair-faced concrete / Color steel plate / Copper plate / Oregon pine half log ; Floor : Terazzo flooring ; Interior Wall : Cloth lining
j. Semba Corporation

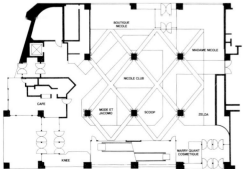

a. 長野東急デパート環境デザイン
b. 長野県長野市
c. 長野東急百貨店
d. ヨコタデザインワークスタジオ　横田良一
e. グッドスピンアーキテクト　房孝
f. 東急百貨店装工部
g. 仲佐写真事務所
h. 柱とアーチにポイントを置き，環境・ショップ，両デザインが共通のテーマ設定のもとに，ルールを設定しクロスオーバーしながら，環境のスケール感・ショップの密度，その互いのメリットを交錯させながらバランスのとれたアイデンティティある商環境を作った．
i. 通路床＝大理石2色パターン貼り／建築柱＝モルタルカキ落し仕上／意匠梁（アーチ）＝シグマルト吹付け
j. ヨコタデザインワークスタジオ／グッドスピンアーキテクト

a. NAGANO TOKYU DEPARTMENT STORE ENVIRONMENT DESIGN
b. Nagano-shi, Nagano
c. Tokyu Department Stor
d. Yokota Design Work Studio Inc. : Ryoichi Yokota
e. Good Spin Architect Inc. : Takashi Fusa
f. Interior Design & Decoration Dept. ; Tokyu Department Store
g. T. Nacasa & Partners
h. A creation of a well-balanced commercial environment having identity by setting up a rule and crossing over, under the common established theme, both the designs of environment and shops with special emphasis on the pillars and arches, as well as blending the individual merits of the sense of environment scale and the density of shopping.
i. Walkway floor : Marble two color pattern flooring ; Architectural pillar : Cement scraping finish ; Arch : Sand coat spraying
j. Yokota Design Work Studio Inc. / Good Spin Architect Inc.

a. ディッコリーファーム
b. 埼玉県川越市
c. サンリオ
d. 岡崎雄三
e. 奥了次／舟貝英伸／小松俊光
f. 船場
h. 各店舗の情景・顔を大切に，楽しい時間と空間をクリエ
   イトし，"ショップロード構想" を展開．
i. サイディングボード吹付タイル／磁器タイル
j. 船場

a. DICKORY FARM
b. Kawagoe-shi, Saitama
c. Inc. Sanrio
d. Yuzo Okazaki
e. Ryoji Oku, Hidenobu Funagai, Toshimitsu Komatsu
f. Semba Corporation
h. A development of a "shopping road concept" by creating
   a pleasant time and space with care taken of the
   landscape and the face of each shop.
i. Siding board spray-on tile / Porcelain tile
j. Semba Corporation

a. 妙香園栄店（茶店）
b. 愛知県名古屋市
c. 妙香園
d. 犬飼芳夫
e. 犬飼芳夫／井上千保子／青木慶子／杉本庄司／建築設計＝松下建築設計事務所
f. 鹿島建設
g. 中部フォトサービス
h. 妙香園のイメージポリシーの拠点化をねらい，話題性の高い和風モダン高感性の商環境の創造．
i. 外装＝ステンレス鏡面，黒ミカゲ／内装＝ミカゲ，タイル，ブロンズミラー
j. 綜合デザインセンター

a. MYOKOEN
b. Nagoya-shi, Aichi
c. Myokoen
d. Yoshio Inukai
e. Yoshio Inukai, Chihoko Inoue, Keiko Aoki, Syoji Sugimoto / Building Plan ; Matsushita Kenchiku Sekkei
f. Kajima Corporation
g. Chubu Photo Service Co., Ltd.
h. A creation of a commercial environment, having a high sense in a Japanese style modernism of full of topics, with the establishment of the image policy of Myokoen aimed at.
i. Exterior facing : Stainless steel mirror finish / Black granite ; Interior : Granite / Tile / Bronze mirror
j. Sogo Design Center

a. カフェレストラン　その
b. 愛知県名古屋市
c. 河合昇
d. 犬飼芳夫
e. 犬飼芳夫／山中博美
f. 光英建設／インテリア水野
g. 中部フォトサービス
h. 店舗は都市景観を構成するに不可欠の要素，その地域の生活文化向上のための提案型店舗．
i. 外装＝タイル (INAX)，カーブドガラス／内装＝床樹脂タイル
j. 綜合デザインセンター

a. CAFE RESTAURANT SONO
b. Nagoya-shi, Aichi
c. Noboru Kwai
d. Yoshio Inukai
e. Yoshio Inukai, Hiromi Yamanaka
f. Koei Kensetsu Co., Ltd.
g. Chubu Photo Service Co., Ltd.
h. Shops are indispensable elements in constituting urban landscape. A suggestion of shops for improving the life culture of the regional area.
i. Exterior facing : Tile (INAX) / Curved glass ; Interior : Resin tile flooring
j. Sogo Design Center

a. 享美術
b. 栃木県益子町
c. 小野沢享子
d. 西山正幸
e. 西山正幸／小倉孝夫
f. 大裕建設
g. 半井孝
h. 建物は固有の土地にある限り，その光，空気，動植物，
　　いわゆる環境と相互応答する．
i. スレート／アルミ板／スチール／ガラス　etc.
j. 西山正幸　昂工房

a. KYO ARTS & CRAFTS
b. Mashiko-machi, Tochigi
c. Kyoko Onozawa
d. Masayuki Nishiyama
e. Masayuki Nishiyama, Takao Ogura
f. Ohiro Kensetsu
g. Takashi Nakarai
h. As far as a building stay at a proper eatate, the building
　　and its environment such as light, air, animals and
　　plants modulate each other. At the site hundred times.
i. Slate / Aluminum plate / Steel / Glass / Others
j. Bau Technic

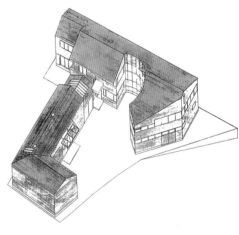

a. レストラン「メープル」
b. 山口県宇部市
c. 上野運輸商会
d. 大昌工芸開発センター
e. 松山一弥／田原昌憲
f. 大昌工芸
g. マツムラフォト
h. アーリーアメリカン調のイメージを基本とし，明るく，白で統一．
i. 壁面＝センチュリーボードVP塗装／屋根＝コロニアル
j. 大昌工芸

a. RESTAURANT "MAPLE"
b. Ube-shi, Yamaguchi
c. Ueno Transport Company
d. Taisho Kogei Co., Ltd. ; Design Development Center
e. Kazuya Matsuyama, Masanori Tahara
f. Taisho Kogei Co., Ltd.
g. Matsumura Photo
h. On the basis of the image of early American, the coloration ot the building adheres to white for brightness.
i. Wall : VP coating on century board ; Roof : Colonial
j. Taisho Kogei Co., Ltd.

a. 飲茶レストラン
b. 東京都墨田区
c. 世新商事
d. 飯田修市
e. 飯田修市
f. 小林工芸社
g. 小松好雄
h. 本場の調理人による本場の味を気軽に楽しんでもらう空間とした.
i. ナラ材／プラスター／大理石／タイル
j. 小林工芸社

a. CHINESE RESTAURANT
b. Sumida-ku, Tokyo
c. Seishin Shoji Corp.
d. Shuichi Iida
e. Shuichi Iida
f. Kobayashi Kogeisha Co., Ltd.
g. Yoshio Komatsu
h. The intention of the design is a creation of a space where one can enjoy one's fill the taste of the genuine cooking by the cooks from where it is cooked.
i. Japanese oakwood / Plaster / Marble / Tile
j. Kobayashi Kogeisha Co., Ltd.

a. **プールホール**
b. 大阪府大阪市
c. プールホール　川村達三
d. 玄子邦治
e. 玄子邦治／丹司典孝
f. ノミック
g. 出合明

h. ほの暗さを基調とした店内は，テーブルがあたかも舞台におけるスポットライトのようなムードだ．
i. アイアンフェイス／Pタイル／VP塗装
j. ノミック

a. POOL HALL
b. Osaka-shi, Osaka
c. Pool Hall : Tatsuzo Kawamura
d. Kuniharu Gengo
e. Kuniharu Gengo, Noritaka Tanji
f. Nomic Co., Ltd.
g. Akira Deai
h. The building interior with a dim lighting as the underlying tone brings about a mood making one feel as if the tables are spot-lighted on a stage.
i. Iron face / P tile / VP coating
j. Nomic Co., Ltd.

a. コットンクラブ   a. COTTON CLUB
b. 新潟県三条市   b. Sanjo-shi, Niigata
c. コットンクラブ   c. Cotton Club
d. 刈屋剛   d. GO Kariya
e. 刈屋剛   e. GO Kariya
f. アスカデザイン室   f. Asuka Inc.
g. 刈屋剛   g. GO Kariya
j. アスカデザイン室   j. Asuka Inc.

a. ブラッセリー　エール
b. 台湾台北市
c. 呉四宝
d. ヨコタデザインワークスタジオ　横田良一
e. ヨコタデザインワークスタジオ　小柴順二
　　設計協力＝SPASSO STUDIO　浜村悟
　　グラフィック＝VIA BO RINK　石川恭子
f. 孫祥福
g. 仲佐写真事務所
i. 床＝御影石貼一部フローリング貼分／壁＝漆喰塗
j. ヨコタデザインワークスタジオ

a. BRASSERIE I'R
b. Taipei-shi, Taiwan
c. S.P. Wo
d. Yokota Design Work Studio Inc.
e. Yokota Design Work Studio Inc. : Junji Koshiba / Spasso
　　Studio : Satoru Hamamura / Via Bo Rink : Kyoko Ishik-
　　awa
f. S.F. Son
g. T. Nacasa & Partner
i. Floor : Granite boarding with flooring partly boarded ;
　　Wall : Plastering
j. Yokota Design Work Studio Inc.

a. 瀬美麻（セピア）
b. 東京都台東区
c. 君塚祥子
d. 高橋直紀
e. 柳田健一／秋本均
f. エンジニアリングフジ
h. 今様日本の美，日本文化の枠と間を今日的スタイルにて
　表現．
i. 小玉石洗い出し／モザイクタイル貼り／モルタル金ゴテ仕
　上OP塗装
j. エンジニアリングフジ

a. CAFE HOUSE SEPIA
b. Taito-ku, Tokyo
c. Yoshiko Kimizuka
d. Naoki Takahashi
e. Kenichi Yanagida, Hitoshi Akimoto
f. Engineering Fuji Co., Ltd.
h. Contemporary beauty of Japan. A frame and interval of
　Japanese culture have been expressed in a contempo-
　rary style.
i. Aggregate exposed finishing by washing / Mosaic tile
　setting / OP painting on cement plastering finish
j. Engineering Fuji Co., Ltd.

a. 萩原宗美容室川崎店
b. 神奈川県川崎市
c. 萩原宗美容室
d. 玉置朝男　ジャパンアートプランニングセンター
e. 玉置朝男／アシスタントデザイナー＝前田和彦
f. 日本建築企画
g. 大東正巳
h. ファッションビルの最も奥まった位置にあるため，導入部のアポイントを明確に表現．
i. スリガラスフッソ処理／ミラーフッソ処理／壁＝VP吹付／床＝Pタイル貼り
j. ジャパンアートプランニングセンター

a. HAGIWARA SO BIYOUSHITSU KAWASAKI
b. Kawasaki-shi, Kanagawa
c. Hagiwara So Biyoshitsu
d. Japan Art Planning Center Co., Ltd. Asao Tamaki
e. Asao Tamaki, Kazuhiko Maeda
f. Nihon Kenchiku Kikaku
g. Masami Daito
h. Located at a deepest spot of the fashion building, the appointments in the approach have been distinctly expressed.
i. Fluorine treated ground glass / Mirror fluorine treated ; Wall : VP spraying ; Floor : P tile flooring
j. Japan Art Planning Center Co., Ltd.

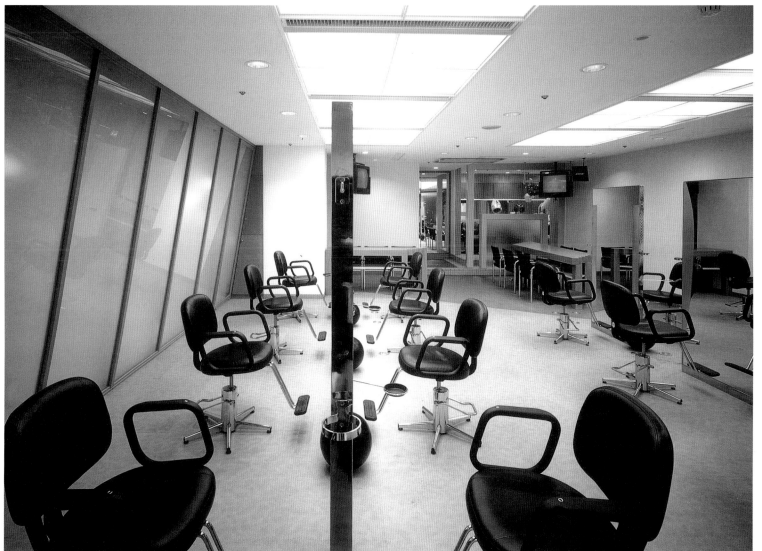

173

a. ブックバーン
b. 愛知県豊橋市
c. ブックバーン
d. 田中健夫
e. 野口隆
f. エンジニアリングフジ
h. 書籍を中心にレコード, 文具などの販売とビデオレンタル
　業務を扱うロードサイドビジネス店舗.
i. AK パネル／カラー鉄板／テラゾーブロック
j. エンジニアリングフジ

a. BOOK BAHN
b. Toyohashi-shi, Aichi
c. Book Bahn Co., Ltd.
d. Takeo Tanaka
e. Takashi Noguchi
f. Engineering Fuji Co., Ltd.
h. A roadside business shop which deals with the sale of
　books as a principal commodity together with records
　and stationery and video rental business.
i. AK panel / Color Iron Plate / Terazzo block
j. Engineering Fuji Co., Ltd.

a. ビーワンショップ
b. 東京都港区
c. 日産自動車
d. 高橋直紀
e. 國分利江子
f. エンジニアリングフジ
h. 日産の全く新しい販売戦略にもとづく車「ビーワン」の情報の受信発信基地.
i. 木製フローリング／グラスメッシュ貼り／石綿セメント板 t 6 LEP
j. エンジニアリングフジ

a. BE-1 SHOP
b. Minato-ku, Tokyo
c. Nissan Motors Co., Ltd.
d. Naoki Takahashi
e. Rieko Kokubun
f. Engineering Fuji Co., Ltd.
h. A base for receiving and dispatching messages relating to a new model car "B-one" which has been developed on the basis of the radically new marketing strategy of Nissan.
i. Wood flooring / Glass mesh lining / Asbestos cement board t6LEP
j. Engineering Fuji Co., Ltd.

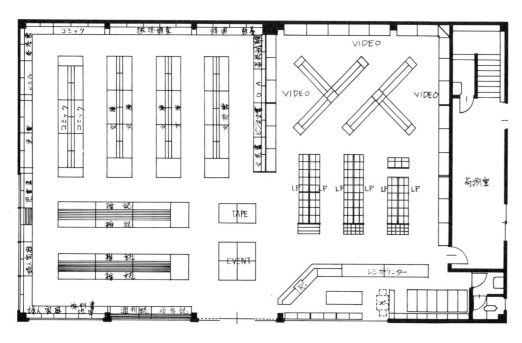

a. メディアコミュニケーションクラブ　すばる
b. 千葉県鎌ケ谷市
c. 村上商事
d. 八百一喜
e. 中原伸光
f. ニッテン
g. 中原伸光
h. 書店とAVレンタルの複合業態に合わせ, カジュアルなス
　タジオのイメージでまとめた.
i. 大波スレート／プラスターボード／VEP ビニールタイル／
　木製什器／スチール什器
j. ニッテン設計事務所, ニッテン

a. MEDIA COMMUNICATION CLUB SUBARU
b. Kamagaya-shi, Chiba
c. Murakami Shogi Co., Ltd.
d. Kazunobu Yao
e. Nobumitsu Nakahara
f. Nitten Co., Ltd.
g. Nobumitsu Nakahara
h. The building has been designed in an image of casual
   studio tailored to the complex business of a book store
   and an AV rental shop.
i. Large corrugated slate / Plaster board / VEP vinyl tile
   / Wood furniture / Steel furniture
j. Nitten Co., Ltd.

a. 文字屋
b. 東京都練馬区
c. 小林工芸社
d. 若林泰佳
e. 弓場哲雄／蟻田晴康
f. ユニオン建装／アドランド工芸
g. 小松好雄
h. 文字に関する全ての MD を取り扱う "文字屋" POP その他の作品商品が展示されやすい店舗構成。
i. ナラ板目染色仕上げ
j. 小林工芸社

a. MOJIYA
b. Nerima-ku, Tokyo
c. Kobayashi Kogeisha Co., Ltd.
d. Yasuyoshi Wakabayashi
e. Tetsuo Yuba, Haruyasu Arita
f. Union Kenso, Adland Kogei
g. Yoshio Komatsu
h. A shop, name of "Mojiya", where all the MDs relating to letters are dealt with. The configuration of the shop is so designed as to allow easy display of POP and other commodities of works.
i. Japanese oakwood grain dyed color finish
j. Kobayashi Kogeisha Co., Ltd.

a. 大阪丸ビル　ビバユー&ヒロミチナカノ
b. 大阪府大阪市
c. もくもく
e. ヨコタデザインワークスタジオ／名取和彦
f. ゼニヤ
g. 仲佐写真事務所

h. 曲線を多用したデザインの中で間接照明によってそれを
　強調し，流れるような客動線を構成した．
i. テラゾ／ナラ材練付染色CL仕上／スチールメラミン焼
　付チヂミ塗装
j. ヨコタデザインワークスタジオ

a. VIVA YOU & HIROMICHI NAKANO
b. Osaka-shi, Osaka
c. Moku des Moku Group
e. Yokota Design Work Studio Inc. : Kazuhiko Natorl
f. Zeniya Co., Ltd.
g. T. Nacasa & Partners

h. A path of flow of customers is structured in the design
　in which many curves by being emphasized in an in-
　direct lighting are used.
i. Terrazzo / Japanese oakwood veneer dyed color LL
　finish / Melamine baking coating crepe finish on steel
j. Yokota Design Work Studio Inc.

a. KIKUYA
b. 北海道札幌市
c. キクヤ
e. SEMBA 設計事務所　ちばまさゆき
f. 船場札幌営業所
g. 安達治

h. イメージへの砦・機能・性能開発が一方的に進められる消費社会に対する反発批判，逆説などの意味を込めて……．
i. 外壁＝PC 板シラー塗装／サイン＝ステンミガキ／床＝舗石300角／壁＝木毛板 EP 塗装
j. SEMBA 設計事務所札幌

a. KIKUYA
b. Sapporo-shi, Hokkaido
c. Kikuya Co., Ltd.
e. Masayuki Chiba
f. Semba Corporation
g. Osamu Adachi
h. The concept implies the resistance, criticism, and para-

dox against the consuming society where the development of a fort for image, function, and performance are one-sidedly promoted.
i. External wall : Sealer coated sign on PC board / Polished stainless steel ; Floor : Paving stone 300 square ; Wall : EP coating on wood wool board
j. Semba Corporation

1F

1BF

a. ブティック ハニーランド
b. 兵庫県姫路市
c. ペップハウス
e. ピクデザイン事務所　山田悦央
f. 三栄建装
g. 宇野穂
h. リニューアルをした外装であり装飾物をとりのぞくことにより大きくみせることができた,
i. 大理石／南洋サクラ材
j. ピクデザイン事務所

a. BOUTIQUE HONEY LAND
b. Himeji-shi, Hyogo
c. PEP House Inc.
e. PC Design Office, Etsuo Yamada
f. Sanei Kenso
g. Minoru Uno
h. A facing which has undergone a renewal and permits itself to look larger by the removal of the decoration.
i. Marble / South sea cherry wood
j. PC Design Office

a. メポビル 2
b. 東京都渋谷区
c. イセキ
d. 井関純夫
e. 清藤元成
f. 片山組
g. 大武秀生
h. 小さくても一戸一戸がはっきりと主張を持つビクトリア期の街並みがコンセプトとなっている.
i. 大理石／石膏モールディング／スウェーデン産ホワイトパイン／人造レンガ
j. イセキ

a. MEPO BLD., 2
b. Shibuya-ku, Tokyo
c. Iseki Co., Ltd.
d. Sumio Iseki
e. Motonari Seito
f. Katayama-gumi Co., Ltd.
g. Hideo Otake
h. The concept is an attempt at representing the street of shops and houses in the Victorian age each of which has its own distinct assertion.
i. Marble / Plaster moulding / White pine from Sweden / Artificial brick
j. Iseki Co., Ltd.

a. 上野丸井　ゼルダ
b. 東京都台東区
c. ニコル
d. ヨコタデザインワークスタジオ　横田良一
e. ヨコタデザインワークスタジオ　富田哲男／設計協力＝
　　伊藤デザイン
f. 美留土
g. 仲佐写真事務所
i. 床＝御影石磨き＆ジェット／棚＝ウレタン塗装，楢材染色
　　仕上
j. ヨコタデザインワークスタジオ

a. UENO MARUI ZELDA
b. Taito-ku, Tokyo
c. Nicole Co., Ltd.
d. Yokota Design Work Studio Inc. : Ryoichi Yokota
e. Yokota Design Work Studio Inc. : Tetsuo Tomita, Ito
　　Design
f. Build Inc.
g. T-Nacasa & Partners
i. Floor : Granite ground and jet finish ; Rack : Urethane
　　coating / Japanese oak dyed color finish
j. Yokota Design Work Studio Inc.

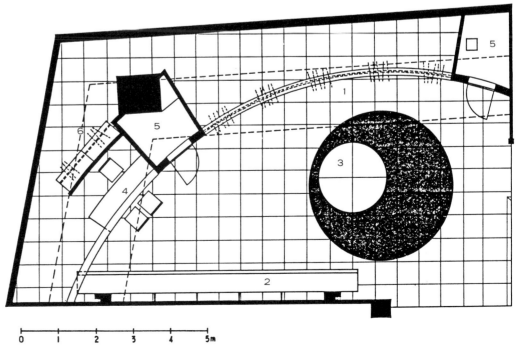

1. HANGER
2. SHELF
3. CO-ORDINATE TABLE
4. COUNTER
5. FITTING ROOM
6. STOCK

0 1 2 3 4 5m

a. 向ケ丘遊園メリーフラワー
b. 神奈川県川崎市
c. 阪和興業
d. 大山忠史
e. 小塚秀忠／中辻伸／原田文雄
f. 乃村工藝社
g. 佐藤喜之
h. "花と緑の遊園地" のセンタープラザに位置するハイビスカスをモチーフにしたシンボリックな遊具.
i. 鉄骨下地・FRP／スチールパイプ・スチールボール／長尺シート／イルミネーション
j. 乃村工藝社

a. MERRY FLOWER
b. Kawasaki-shi, Kanagawa
c. Hanwa Kogyo Co., Ltd.
d. Tadashi Oyama
e. Hidetada Kozuka, Shin Nakatsuji, Fumio Harada
f. Nomura Display Co., Ltd.
g. Yoshiyuki Sato
h. Symbolic playthings with a hybiscus adopted as a motif which is located in the center plaza of the "Recreation ground of flowers and green".
i. FRP on the base of Steel structure / Steel pipe and steel ball / Long length sheet / Illumination
j. Nomura Display Co., Ltd.

a. ムーンビーチ「フロート」
b. 広島県沖美町
c. 防予汽船
d. ひろしま美術研究所／大井健二
e. 大昌工芸／環境デザイン研究所／小池晋弘
f. 大昌工芸
g. ギンレイフォト
j. 大昌工芸

a. MOON BEACH「FLOAT」
b. Okimi-cho, Hiroshima
c. Boyo Kisen Co., Ltd.
d. Hiroshima Art Seminary / Kenji Ohi
e. Taisho Kogei Co., Ltd. / Environmental Design Institute
　/ Nobuhiro Koike
f. Taisho Kogei Co., Ltd.
g. Ginrei Photo
j. Taisho Kogei Co., Ltd.

a. ファサード
b. 静岡県浜松市
c. せつむら
d. ヨコタデザインワークスタジオ　横田良一
e. グッドスピンアーキテクト　井澤久
f. 丸北建設
g. 白鳥美雄
h. 建物の前面にファサードウォールを設け既存の街並みから一線を画し，商環境としての充実を図った．それは内部環境全体として，各ショップの配置的条件の均質化，グレードの統一化を図る意味がある．プロジェクトの進行上SHOPデザインと建築デザインを同時進行させることにより環境をトータルに捉えた，つまりインテリアが建築になったのである．
i. 外壁＝RCコンクリート打放しの上アクアシール塗装／ファサード＝H型鋼＋グレーチングマリンペイント塗装／共用床＝舗石平板コンクリートワックス塗り／壁＝コンクリート打放しⅠ部ガラスブロック／天井＝コンクリート打放し一部石綿スレート板張り
j. ヨコタデザインワークスタジオ／グッドスピンアーキテクト

a. FACADE
b. Hamamatsu-shi, Shizuoka
c. Setsumura
d. Yokota Design Work Studio Inc. : Ryoichi Yokota
e. Good Spin Architect. Inc. : Hisashi Izawa
f. Marukita Kensetsu
g. Yoshio Shiratori
h. By drawing a line of discrimination against the existing street of shops and houses, the scheme attempted to enrich the area as a commercial environment. This implies homogenization and grade unification of the layout condition of each shop when viewed as a whole in terms of interior environment. The scheme grasped the environment in its totality by allowing the shop design and architectural design to concurrently proceed for convenience of promoting the project. This, in other words, is because the interior has taken the place of the architecture.
i. Exterior wall : Aquaseal coating on RC fair-faced concrete ; Facade : Marine paint coating on H shape steel grating ; Common floor : Wax coating on paving stone flat plate concrete ; Wall : Fair-faced concrete and partially glass block ; Ceiling : Fair-faced concrete partially asbestos plate lining
j. Yokota Design Work Studio Inc. / Good Spin Architect Inc.

a. ファサード地下1階 スクープ&クロッシング
b. 静岡県浜松市
c. スクープ
d. ヨコタデザインワークスタジオ　横田良一
e. ヨコタデザインワークスタジオ　鎌田真司
f. ゼニヤ
g. 白鳥美雄
i. 床=(ボーゾー) 木ブロックフローリング／壁=コンクリート
　 打放し、一部壁面十和田石／天井=ケイカル板 CL 仕上
　 げ
j. ヨコタデザインワークスタジオ／グッドスピンアーキテクト

a. FACADE B1F SCOOP & XING
b. Hamamatsu-shi, Shizuoka
c. Scoop Inc.
d. Yokota Design Work Studio Inc. : Ryoichi Yokota
e. Yokota Design Work Studio Inc. : Shinji Kamata
f. Zeniya Co., Ltd.
g. Yoshio Shiratori
i. Floor : Wood block flooring ; Wall : Fair-faced concrete
　 partially wall-surface+Towada-stone ; Ceiling : CL fin-
　 ish on Calcium silicate board
j. Yokota Design Work Studio Inc. / Good Spin Architect
　 Inc.

a. ファサード1階 スクープマン
b. 静岡県浜松市
c. スクープマン
d. ヨコタデザインワークスタジオ　横田良一
e. ヨコタデザインワークスタジオ　富田哲男
f. ゼニヤ
g. 白鳥美雄
i. 床=花櫚フローリングウレタンクリアー／壁=コンクリート
　 打放し、1部特注型使用／天井=PB下地 AEP 塗装仕
　 上げ
j. ヨコタデザインワークスタジオ／グッドスピンアーキテクト

a. FACADE 1F SCOOPMAN
b. Hamamatsu-shi, Shizuoka
c. Scoopman Inc.
d. Yokota Design Work Studio Inc. : Ryoichi Yokota
e. Yokota Design Work Studio Inc. : Tetsuo Tomita
f. Zeniya Co., Ltd.
g. Yoshio Shiratori
i. Floor : urethane clear on Chinese quince wood flooring ;
　 Wall : Fair-faced concrete partially special order mold
　 used ; Ceiling : AEP coating finish on PB rough coating
j. Yokota Design Work Studio Inc. / Good Spin Architect
　 Inc.

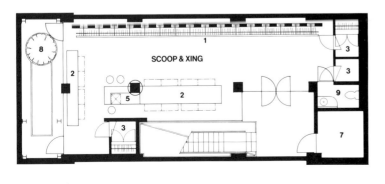

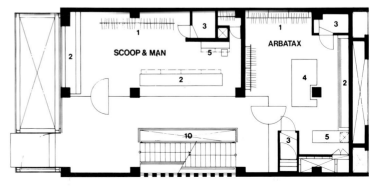

a. ファサード2階 ファサードカフェ
b. 静岡県浜松市
c. 三永
d. ヨコタデザインワークスタジオ　横田良一
e. ヨコタデザインワークスタジオ　名取和彦／設計協力＝
　山口スペースデザイン
f. ゼニヤ
g. 白鳥美雄
i. 床＝黒御影石貼／壁・天井＝在来コンクリート打放し仕
　上（1部目地取り）
j. ヨコタデザインワークスタジオ／グッドスピンアーキテクト

a. FACADE 2F FACADE CAFÉ
b. Hamamatsu-shi, Shizuoka
c. Sun-A Co., Ltd.
d. Yokota Design Work Studio Inc. : Ryoichi Yokota
e. Yokota Design Work Studio Inc. : Kazuhiko Natori
　Yamaguchi Space Design
f. Zeniya Co., Ltd.
g. Yoshio Shiratori
i. Floor : Black granite setting ; Wall & ceiling : Conven-
　tional fair-faced concrete finish (partially joint removed)
j. Yokota Design Work Studio Inc. / Good Spin Architect
　Inc.

a. ファサード3階 ボッシュ＆ヒロミチナカノ
b. 静岡県浜松市
c. 三永
d. ヨコタデザインワークスタジオ　横田良一
e. ヨコタデザインワークスタジオ　名取和彦
f. ゼニヤ
g. 白鳥美雄
i. 床＝イタリアン大理石／壁・天井＝在来コンクリート打放
　し仕上（リブ状）
j. ヨコタデザインワークスタジオ／グッドスピンアーキテクト

a. FACADE 3F BOSH & HIROMICHI NAKANO
b. Hamamatsu-shi, Shizuoka
c. Sun-A Co., Ltd.
d. Yokota Design Work Studio Inc. : Ryoichi Yokota
e. Yokota Design Work Studio Inc. : Kazuhiko Natori
f. Zeniya Co., Ltd.
g. Yoshio Shiratori
i. Floor : Italian marble ; Wall & Ceiling : conventional
　fair-faced concrete finish (ribbed finish)
j. Yokota Design Work Studio Inc. / Good Spin Architect
　Inc.

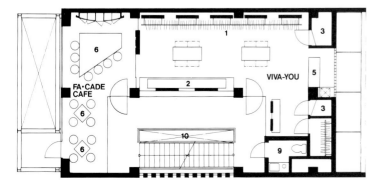

a. **マリンポートコーチヤクラブハウス**
b. 神奈川県横須賀市
c. 高知屋造船所
d. 吉川準治
e. 柳田健一
f. エンジニアリングフジ

h. ボートクルージングから帰港した人々を迎え入れる場。ブレーンで柔らかいボリューム感を意図した。
i. タモ染色／パーケット床材
j. エンジニアリングフジ

a. MARINE PORT KOCHIYA CLUB HOUSE
b. Yokosuka-shi, Kanagawa
c. Kochiya Marine Port Co., Ltd.
d. Junji Yoshikawa
e. Kenichi Yanagida
f. Engineering Fuji Co., Ltd.

h. The place where people returning to the port from their boat-cruising are received. The design of the club house intended to provide plain, soft, and massive feeling.
i. Tamo dyed color / Parket flooring material
j. Engineering Fuji Co., Ltd.

a. 塩沢湖レイクランド
b. 長野県軽井沢町
c. 塩沢遊園
d. GK 設計　朝倉則幸
e. 渡和由／松永博己／岩崎耕一
f. 北野建設
g. 岩為
h. 湖畔の自然を体感する仕掛けをもつリゾート空間．施設の形態と素材が高原の風景と場を印象づける．
i. カラ松／杉／浅間石／スチール
j. GK 設計

a. SIOZAWAKO LAKE LAND
b. Karuizawa-machi Nagano
c. Shiozawa Yuen Co., Ltd.
d. GK Sekkei Associates ; Noriyuki Asakura
e. Kazuyoshi Watari, Hiromi Matsunaga, Kouichi Iwasaki
f. Kitano Construction Corporation
g. Gan Tame
h. A resort space which is designed to allow visitors to bodily sense the nature at the lakeside. The configuration of the facilities and the materials impresses the visitors with the landscape of the plateau and the space.
i. Japanese larch / Japanese cedar / Asama stone / Steel
j. GK Sekkei Associates

a. 塩沢湖レイクランド
b. 長野県軽井沢町
c. 塩沢遊園
d. GK 設計　朝倉則幸
e. 渡和由／松永博己／岩崎耕一
f. 北野建設
g. 岩為

a. SIOZAWAKO LAKE LAND
b. Karuizawa-machi Nagano
c. Shiozawa Yuen Co., Ltd.
d. GK Sekkei Associates ; Noriyuki Asakura
e. Kazuyoshi Watari, Hiromi Matsunaga, Kouichi Iwasaki
f. Kitano Construction Corporation
g. Gan Tame
h. A resort space which is designed to allow visitors to bodily sense the nature at the lakeside. The configuration of the facilities and the materials impresses the visitors with the landscape of the plateau and the space.
i. Japanese larch / Japanese cedar / Asama stone / Steel
j. GK Sekkei Associates

a. CITY SCREEN 4 inner village MIYAMA(増築)
b. 長野県北安曇郡白馬村
c. 矢口公勝
e. 池上俊郎／池上明
f. 守谷商会松本支店
g. ARC STUDIO=畑義温
h. スキーを中心とする屋外スポーツのためのホテル．自然とのふれあいの外部空間を多様化．
i. 外壁=リシン吹付／開口部=アルミサッシ（自然発色）
j. アーバンガウス研究所

a. CITY SCREEN 4 INNER VILLAGE MIYAMA
b. Hakuba-mura, Nagano
c. Koshyo Yaguchi
e. Toshiro Ikegami, Akira Ikegami
f. Moriya Shokai Co., Ltd. Matsumoto-Shiten
g. ARC Studio : Yoshiharu Hata
h. A hotel for outdoor sport players, including principally skiers. The external space, coming in contact with nature, offers a diversified appearance.
i. Wall : Lysine spray on ; Opening part : Aluminum sash (natural coloring)
j. Urbangauss

a. 東洋ホテル　リノベーション
b. 大阪府大阪市
c. 東洋ホテル
d. プロデューサー＝東畑建築事務所（谷淳之介，本持一博）／アートディレクター・店舗＝高島屋（岡崎敬三）／アートディレクター・店舗・サイン＝乃村工藝社（西垣雅弘，楠山和人，木屋久男）／アートディレクター・照明＝ライズライティングデザイン（岡幸男）
e. 設計・監理＝大林組（田澤道生，山田浩）
f. 大林組
g. 東洋ホテル写真館　大熊操
h. イメージテーマを日本文化の基点である「シルクロード」としてデザインの展開を図っている．
i. 床＝大理石（トラバーチン），カーペット／壁＝大理石（トラバーチン）
j. 大林組本店設計第2部

a. TOYO HOTEL RENOVATION
b. Osaka-shi, Osaka
c. Toyo Hotel Ltd.
d. K. Tohata & Associates Architects : Junnoshuke Tani, Kazuhiro Motomochi / ohbayashi-Gumi, Ltd. : Michio Tazawa, Hiroshi Yamada / Takashimaya Co., Ltd. : Keizo Okazaki / Nomura Display Co., Ltd. : Masahiro Nishigaki, Kazuto Kusuyama, Hisao Kiya / Rise Lighting Design : Yukio Oka
f. Ohbayashi-Gumi, Ltd.
g. Toyo Hotel Photographer : Misao Okuma
h. The concept attempted to develop the design with "Silk Road", the original point of Japanese culture, as a theme of the image.
i. Flooring : Marble (artificial marble) / Carpet ; Wall : Marble (Artificial marble)
j. Ohbayashi-Gumi, Ltd.

a. ホテル日航アンヌプリ
b. 北海道虻田郡ニセコ町
c. ホテル日航アンヌプリ
d. 佐野幸夫
e. 上野卓二／寺島振介／豊田幸夫
f. 鹿島建設
g. 新津写真
h. ゲレンデに直結したホテルで，除雪の問題を考慮しつつ，既存の樹木を景観として生かした．
i. 植栽＝シラカバ，ナナカマド，トドマツ
j. 鹿島建設建築設計本部

a. HOTEL NIKKO ANNUPRI
b. Niseko-machi, Hokkaido
c. Hotel Nikko Annupri Co., Ltd.
d. Yukio Sano
e. Takuji Ueno, Shinsuke Terashima, Yukio Toyoda
f. Kajima Corporation
g. Niitsu Photo Studio
h. A hotel allowing a direct access to the skiing slope, where the existing trees are made efficient use of for landscaping with the problem of snow-removing taken into consideration.
i. Planting : White birch / Rowan tree / Abies
j. Kajima Corporation

a. 諏訪ゴルフ倶楽部クラブハウス
b. 長野県諏訪市
c. ヘルシィリゾート
e. 佐々木治行
f. 大成建設
g. SS 名古屋
h. 3連の屋根が，周囲の山並と連なり，清々しさを感じさせ
るデザインに留意した．
i. カラー鉄板平葺／有機質砂状塗料吹付／天然石割肌
貼
j. 大成建設設計本部

a. SUWA GOLF CLUB ; CLUB HOUSE
b. Suwa-shi, Nagano
c. Healthy Resort Inc.
e. Haruyuki Sasaki
f. Taisei Corporation
g. SS Nagoya Inc.
h. Consideration has been given to the design of the house
where a refreshing feeling is offered with its three
ranges of roofs modulated to the encompassing mountain ranges.
i. Colored iron plate flat roofing / Organic sandy coat
spraying / Broken-natural-stone setting
j. Taisei Corporation

a. セソール川崎京町ハイライズ
b. 神奈川県川崎市
c. 興和不動産
d. 長谷川工務店　松浪秀晴
e. デザイン＝空間工房，太田清一／設計＝長谷川工務店，
　 河村順二
f. 長谷川工務店
g. 創芸
h. ゲートは時代と情報のウェイブをモチーフとし，モニュメン
　 トは人間の手をイメージした.
i. コンクリート打放し／ステンレスパイプ／御影石
j. 長谷川工務店

a. SESOHL KAWASAKI KYOMACHI HIGHRISE
b. Kawasaki-shi, Kanagawa
c. Kowa Fudosan Co., Ltd.
d. Hasegawa Komuten Co., Ltd. : Hideharu Matsunami
e. Design : Kukan Kobo : Kiyokazu Ota / Planning : Haseg-
　 awa Komuten Co., Ltd. : Junji Kawamura
f. Hasegawa Komuten Co., Ltd.
g. Sogei Co., Ltd.
h. The gate uses the waves of the times and information
　 as its motif, while the monument images the humane
　 hands.
i. Fair-faced concrete / Stainless steel pipe / Granite
j. Hasegawa Komuten Co., Ltd.

a. 三井不動産パークシティー新川崎第二番街，セントラルアベニュー
b. 神奈川県川崎市
c. 三井不動産
d. 三井不動産／中島幹夫
e. 鹿島建設建築設計本部:上野卓二，緒方基秀，三木正／三井建設設計部:福本康裕／葛貫武／彫刻=中島幹夫

f. 鹿島建設
g. 五十嵐潔
h. 街の個性を象徴するセントラルアベニューの彫刻．人のふれあいをテーマとした彫刻．コナラ，エゴノキを見ながら走るジョギングロード，など住環境のアイデンティティーをテーマとした．
j. 鹿島建設建築設計本部

a. RARK CITY SHINKAWASAKI
b. Kawasaki-shi, Kanagawa
c. Mitsui Real Estate Development
d. Mitsui Real Estate Development : Mikio Nakajima
e. Kajima Corporation : Takuji Ueno, Motohide Ogata, Tadashi, Miki / Mitsui Corporation Co., Ltd. : Yasuhiro Fukumoto, Takeshi Tsuzuranuki
f. Kajima Corporation

g. Kiyoshi Igarashi
h. The scheme uses the identity of the living environment as a theme. This scheme includes a jogging road along which people run as wathing trees, such as thunbs and styracaceaes, and sculptures which express as a theme a contact between people and the sculptures of the Central Avenue that symbolize the identity of the city.
j. Kajima Corporation

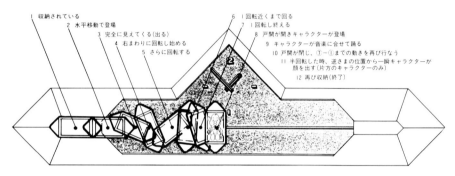

1 収納されている
2 水平移動で登場
3 完全に見えてくる(出る)
4 右まわりに回転し始める
5 さらに回転する

6 1回転近くまで回る
7 1回転し終える
8 戸開が開きキャラクターが登場
9 キャラクターが音楽に合せて踊る
10 戸開が閉じ、(7)〜(1)までの動きを再び行なう
11 半回転した時、逆さまの位置から一瞬キャラクターが顔を出す(片方のキャラクターのみ)
12 再び収納(終了)

a. 京阪モールクロック
b. 大阪府大阪市
c. 京阪電鉄商事／服部セイコー
d. 鏡味賢二
e. 鏡味賢二
f. 乃村工藝社
h. 未来環境をイメージさせる時計の中をカプセルが左右に移動し、さらにキャラクターが登場する。
j. 乃村工藝社

a. KEIHAN MALL CLOCK
b. Osaka-shi, Osaka
c. Keihan Dentetsu Corporation／Hattori Seiko
d. Kenji Kagami
e. Kenji Kagami
f. Nomura Display Co., Ltd.
h. Two characters, riding in each capsule, make an entrance from left to right on the stage in the clock which images future environment.
j. Nomura Display Co., Ltd.

a. ジャスコ新茨木店
b. 大阪府茨木市
c. ジャスコ
d. 岡西昭雄／山本忠夫
e. 玉置喜久／池田忠／からくり時計＝大森達郎
f. 船場／間組

g. 福本正明
h. からくり時計が時をきざむと，子供がセントラルコートいっ
　 ぱいに集まる話題性のある明るい空間．
i. ハーフミラー／ステンレス／FRP
j. 船場

a. JUSCO SHIN IBARAKI
b. Ibaraki-shi, Osaka
c. JUSCO
d. Akio Okanishi, Tadao Yamamoto
e. Yoshihisa Tamaki, Tadashi Ikeda, Tatsuro Omori
f. Semba Corporation ; Hazama-gumi

g. Masaaki Hukumoto
h. A bright space with an ample stock of topics where
　 children get gathered as filling up the central court
　 when the gimmick clock strikes the hour.
i. Half mirror / Stainless steel / FRP
j. Semba Corporation

a. 鶴見駅西口バスシェルター
b. 神奈川県横浜市
c. 横浜市
d. 西沢健／宮沢功
e. 斉藤恭助／田中一雄
f. リバースチール
g. 仲佐写真事務所
h. 幾何学的な形態を連続的に展開することによって，波の
　　イメージを光の回廊として表現した．
i. ポリカーボネート／H型鋼／スチール丸パイプ
j. GK 設計

a. TURUMI STATION WEST SIDE BUS SHELTER
b. Yokohama-shi, Kanagawa
c. City of Yokohama
d. Takeshi Nishizawa, Isao Miyazawa
e. Kyosuke Saito, Kazuo Tanaka
f. River Steel
g. T.Nacasa & Partners
h. The continuous development of geometric configura-
　　tions expresses the image of waves of the sea as a
　　corridor of light.
i. Polycarbonate / H-shape beam / steel round pipe
j. GK Sekkei Associates

a. 横浜駅西口バス停上家改修工事
b. 神奈川県横浜市
c. 横浜駅西口周辺地区整備協議会
e. 横総合計画事務所／大林組東京本社一級建築士事務
　所
f. 大林組東京本社
g. クドウ・フォト
h. この計画は，広場のもつボキャブラリーに従い，調和のと
　れたデザインで，広場の風景に溶け込む。
i. 鉄骨（H鋼・丸鋼）／ポリカーボネート板（高耐候性処
　理）／RC打放し小たたき
j. 大林組東京本社設計第二部

a. BUS STOP IN WEST PLAZA YOKOHAMA CEN-
　TRAL STATION
b. Yokohama-shi, Kanagawa
e. Maki and Associates / Ohbayashi-Gumi, Ltd.; Tokyo
　Head Office, Architects and Engineers
f. Ohbayashi-Gumi, Ltd.; Tokyo Head Office
g. Kudo Photo
h. The scheme, following the vocabulary the square has,
　attempts to harmoniously design the station so that the
　station is modulated to the landscape of square.
i. Steel frame (H-shape beam / Round bar steel) /
　Polycarbonate plate (High Weatherproof treatment) /
　Fair-faced RC dabbed finish
j. Ohbayashi Gumi, Ltd.

a. 大阪サインタワー
b. 大阪府大阪市（市境付近10ヵ所）
c. 大阪市＋大阪市土木技術協会
d. 花輪恒
e. 森田昌嗣／中井川正道
f. 日本鉄塔工業
g. 仲佐写真事務所
h. ゲートサインとして市内のサインシステムと連携し，都市
　の領域を顕在化している.
i. ステンレス／アルミ合金鋳物／耐候性鋼
j. GK 設計

a. OSAKA SIGN TOWER
b. 10 Places around the city boundaries of Osaka
c. The City of Osaka
d. Hisashi hanawa
e. Yoshitsugu Morita, Masamichi Nakaigawa
f. Japan Steel Tower Company
g. T. Nacasa & Partners
h. As a gate sign, the Osaka Sign Tower visualizes what
   are happening in the territory of the city by acting in
   concert with the sign system of the city.
i. Stainless steel / Aluminum alloy casting / Weatherproof steel
j. GK Sekkei Associates

a. 第7回玉川 "自然・ひと・対話" 展
b. 東京都世田谷区
c. 玉川高島屋 S.C.
d. 瀬口英徳
e. 瀬口英徳
f. エンジニアリングフジ
h. 異種素材の混入によって，新たな演出力を与えられたテラゾーの光ファイバーとの融合作品．
i. テラミックス／光ファイバー　等
j. エンジニアリングフジ

a. LIGHTEN'86
b. Setagaya-ku, Tokyo
c. Tamagawa Takashimaya S.C.
d. Hidenori Seguchi
e. Hidenori Seguchi
f. Engineering Fuji Co., Ltd.
h. A work in which optical fibers act in good harmony with the terrazzo which provides a new stage effect by the help of the mixture of the different kinds of materials.
i. Terramix / Optical fiber / Others
j. Engineering Fuji Co., Ltd.

a. 桐陽台「モニュメント」
b. 広島県広島市
c. 有楽土地
d. アクラ環境設計／熊本光三
e. 大昌工芸環境デザイン研究所，小池晋弘，若林誠
f. みずえ緑地
g. ギンレイフォト
h. 新興団地の導入路に位置し，そこに住む人々の「平和と協調性」をシンボリックに表現.
i. コンクリート／部分的にはモザイクタイル／FRP
j. 大昌工芸

a. TOYODAI "MONUMENT"
b. Hiroshima-shi, Hiroshima
c. Uraku Land Co., Ltd.
d. UCLA Urban Design : Mitsuzo Kumamoto
e. Taisho Kogei Co., Ltd. ; Environmental Design Institute Nobuhiro Koike / Makoto Wakabayashi
g. Ginrei Photo
h. The monument located at a side of the approach road to the newly developed housing area symbolically expresses the "Peace and Cooperativeness" of the inhabitants there.
i. Concrete / Partial mosaic tile / FRP (Fiberglass Reinforced Plastics)
j. Taisho Kogei Co., Ltd.

a. 小野田中央公園「噴水モニュメント」
b. 山口県小野田市
c. 小野田市都市計画課
d. 大昌工芸環境デザイン研究所
e. 設計＝小池晋弘，法安史郎／モニュメント＝日田敦子
f. 長沢建設／大昌工芸
g. ギンレイフォト
h. 外構に休憩スペースと花壇を兼用させ，市民の「憩いと集いの場」として演出. モニュメントは光り輝く未来を表現.
i. ステンレス／花崗岩／FRP
j. 大昌工芸

a. ONODA CENTRAL PARK "FOUNTAIN MONUMENT"
b. Onoda-shi, Yamaguchi
c. Onoda-shi / Urban Planning Dept.
d. Taisho Kogei Co., Ltd. ; Environmental Design Institute
e. Planning : Nobuhiro Koike, Shiro Houan / Monument : Atsuko Hita
f. Nagasawa Construction Co., Ltd. ; Taisho Kogei Co., Ltd.
g. Ginrei Photo
h. The monument expresses a brilliant future, in the surrounding of which there is presented a space for a rest combined with a flower bed as a place for "repose and gathering".
i. Stainless steel / Grenite / FRP (Fiberglass Reinforced Plastics)
j. Taisho Kogei Co., Ltd.

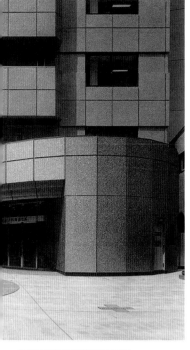

a. 名古屋駅前日興プラザ「にこにこタワー」
b. 愛知県名古屋市
c. 日興ビルディング
d. 三菱地所第二建築部
e. 榎本建規／三菱地所第二建築部 (川上雅靖)
f. 乃村工藝社
g. SS 名古屋
h. 名古屋駅前日興證券ビルの公開空地に設置された国際性と風土性をメインテーマとする時計塔.
i. ネオパリエ／FRP 成形 (ゴールド・彩色)／真鍮ステンレス HL
j. 三菱地所

a. "NIKONIKO TOWER" AT NAGOYA EKIMAE NIKKO PLAZA
b. Nagoya-shi, Aichi
c. Nikko Building Co., Ltd.
d. Mitsubishi Estate Co., Ltd.
e. Takemi Enomoto / Mitsubishi Estate Co., Ltd. : Masayasu Kawakami
f. Nomura Display
g. SS Nagoya
h. A clock tower that stands in the open vacant lot of the Nikko Securities building in front of the Nagoya Station, using internationalism and cooperative attitude as a main theme.
i. Neopalier (artificial marble) / FRP formation (gold coloring) / Brass / Stainless steel
j Mitsubishi Estate Co., Ltd.

a. 中央公園「時計塔」
b. 広島県呉市
c. 呉市都市計画課
d. LAT 環境設計事務所
e. 青木成夫
f. 大昌工芸
g. ギンレイフォト
h. 明るい未来に向って前進する呉市の姿をシンボリックに表現.
i. ステンレス
j. 大昌工芸

a. CENTRAL PARK "MEMOREAL TOWER"
b. Kure-shi, Hiroshima
c. Kure-shi, Urban Planning Dept.
d. LAT Environmental Design Office
e. Nario Aoki
f. Taisho Kogei Co., Ltd.
g. Ginrei Photo
h. The tower symbolically expresses a picture of Kure City who proceeds toward a bright future.
i. Stainless steel
j. Taisho Kogei Co., Ltd.

a. アトリオ・クロック
b. 石川県金沢市
c. 香林坊・アトリオ
d. 遠藤英雄
e. 杉山知生／楠目克美／人形デザイン＝金子清二／音楽＝小泉正美
f. 服部セイコー／乃村工藝社
g. 大東正巳
h. アシリウムを"広場"と考え，広場に現われる大道芸人をテーマとし，柱時計としての形を心掛けた．
i. 鋼板焼き付け塗装／真鍮／人形＝FRP樹脂
j. 乃村工藝社

a. ATRIO CLOCK
b. Kanazawa-shi, Ishikawa
c. Korinbo Atrio
d. Hideo Endo
e. Tomoo Sugiyama, Katsumi Kusume, Seiji Kaneko Masami Koizumi
f. Nomura Display Co., Ltd. : Hattori Seiko
g. Masami Daito
h. The concept is an attempt at forming the clock after a wall clock, using as a theme a street performer appearing in the atrium as assuming it to be a square.
i. Baking paint on steel plate / Brass / Puppet-FRP resin
j. Nomura Display Co., Ltd.

アトリオ・クロック
石川県金沢市
香林坊・アトリオ
遠藤英雄
杉山知生／楠目克美／人形デザイン＝金子清二／音楽＝小泉正美
服部セイコー／乃村工藝社
大東正巳
アシリウムを"広場"と考え，広場に現われる大道芸人をテーマとし，柱時計としての形を心掛けた．
鋼板焼き付け塗装／真鍮／人形＝FRP樹脂
乃村工藝社

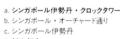

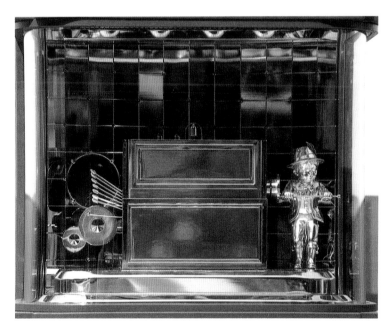

a. シンガポール伊勢丹・クロックタワー
b. シンガポール・オーチャード通り
c. シンガポール伊勢丹
d. 杉山知生
e. 杉山知生／音楽＝小泉正美
f. 服部セイコー／乃村工藝社
g. 山下幸光
h. 時計塔の中に，ショーウインドとしての美しさを持たせ，一つのモニュメントとして表現した．
i. 鋼板焼き付け塗装／真鍮／ガラス／人形＝FRP樹脂金箔ばり
j. 乃村工藝社

a. SINGAPORE ISETAN CLOCK TOWER
b. Orchard Road, Singapore
c. Singapore Isetan
d. Tomoo Sugiyama
e. Tomoo Sugiyama, Masami Koizumi
f. Nomura Display Co., Ltd. : Hattori Seiko
g. Yukimitsu Yamashita
h. The clock tower is expressed as a monument with a beauty of show window provided in the tower.
i. Baking paint on steel plate / Brass / Glass / Puppet-FRP resin plated with gold foil
j. Nomura Display Co., Ltd.

a. 名古屋ターミナルビル "テリヨン"
b. 愛知県名古屋市
c. 名古屋ターミナルビル
d. 遠藤英雄
e. 杉山知生／楠目克美／人形デザイン＝伊藤尚志／イラストレーター＝高宮邦彦
f. 服部セイコー／乃村工藝社
g. 大東正巳
h. 名古屋の名物・名所を１枚のイラストマップにまとめ，その中より人形を登場させ，演出した．
i. ステンレス・ヘアライン・エッチング仕上げ／鋼板焼き付け塗装／人形＝FRP樹脂
j. 乃村工藝社

a. NAGOYA TERMINAL BUILDING "TERIYON"
b. Nagoya-shi, Aichi
c. Nagoya Terminal Co., Ltd.
d. Hideo Endo
e. Tomoo Sugiyama, Katsumi Kusume, Hisashi Ito, Kunihiko Takamiya
f. Hattori Seiko, Nomura Display Co., Ltd.
g. Masami Daito
h. The clock tower presents one surface of an illustration map in which the noted products and noted places in Nagoya have been brought together with puppets allowed to appear on the surface.
i. Stainless steel with the surface line etching finished / Baking paint on steel plate / Puppet-FRP resin
j. Nomura Display Co., Ltd.

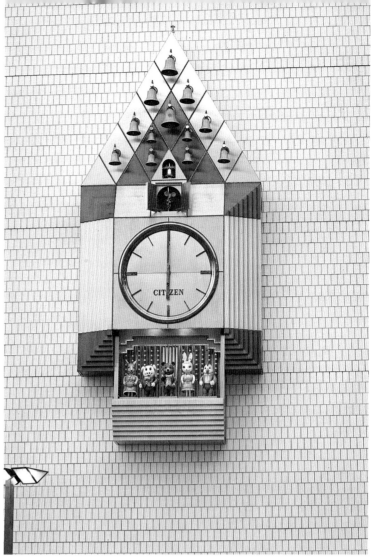

a. 小田急カリヨン時計
b. 東京都新宿区
c. 小田急百貨店／シチズン商事
d. 吉田慧
e. 池上典・エンバイロン
f. TIC・CITIZN ／アルス／昭和ネオン／日本楽器
h. 毎正時になると時計の中から，5匹の動物がカリヨンを
　演奏して，街行く人に刻を知らせます．
j. アルス HED 事業部

a. ODAKYU CARILLON CLOCK
b. Shinjuku-ku, Tokyo
c. Odakyu Department Store, Cetizen Trading
d. Satoshi Yoshida
e. Environ : Nori Ikegami
f. TIC Citizen ; Arusu Co., Ltd. ; Showa Neon ; Nippon Gakki
h. At every noon, five animals play the carillon in the clock, chiming the hour for the passersby in the street.
j. Arusu Co., Ltd.

a. ワンダーボール　スカルプチャー
b. 北海道滝川市
c. 西友
d. 関口敏美
e. 関口デザイン研究所
f. 小林工芸社
g. 越信義
i. 鋼管材／アクリル樹脂／ネオン
j. 小林工芸社

a. WONDER BALL SCULPTURE
b. Takikawa-shi, Hokkaido
c. Seiyu Co., Ltd.
d. Toshimi Sekiguchi
e. Sekiguchi Design Institute
f. Kobayashi kogeisha Co., Ltd.
g. Nobuyoshi Koshi
i. Steel pipes / Acrylate resin / Neon
j. Kobayashi Kogeisha Co., Ltd.

a. ボールクロック
b. 埼玉県春日部市
c. ロビンソン・ジャパン
d. 友田修
e. 池村明生
f. アルス HED 事業部
h. 毎正時になると，時計の下のレール上に，ボールが転がり，チャイムを鳴らして刻を知らせます．
j. アルス HED 事業部

a. BALL CLOCK
b. Kasukabe-shi, Saitama
c. Robinson's Japan
d. Osamu Tomoda
e. Akio Ikemura
f. Arusu Co., Ltd.
h. At every noon, a ball rolls down on the rail beneath the clock, chiming the hour.
j. Arusu Co., Ltd.

a. 静岡・伝馬町再開発ビル
b. 静岡県静岡市
c. 伝馬町プラザ　加藤次郎作
e. 設計監理＝針谷建築事務所／ストリートインテリア＝神成澪
f. 安藤・木内共同企業体
g. アトリエ飯嶋
h. 緑のショッピングモールを持った複合施設.
i. 外装＝現場打レリーフ／メタリック吹付タイル
j. 針谷建築事務所

a SHIZUOKA-TENMA-CHO RE-DEVELOPMENT
　BUILDING
b. Shizuoka-shi, Shizuoka
c. Tenma-cho Plaza : Jirosaku Kato
e. Planning : Harigaya Architect Office / Shizu Kaminari
f. Ando-Kiuchi, Co., Ltd.
g. Atorie Iijima
h. A complex development having a green shopping mall.
i. Exterior : Relief set on site / Metallic spraying on tile
j. Harigaya Architect Office

a. 壁面装飾
b. 東京都練馬区
c. 西友
d. 田中一光
e. 秋山育／広村正章
f. 小林工芸社
g. 小松好雄
i. カッティングシート
j. 小林工芸社

a. WALL DISPLAY
b. Nerina-ku, Tokyo
c. Seiyu Co., Ltd.
d. Ikko Tanaka
e. Iku Akiyama / Masaaki Hiromura
f. Kobayashi kogeisha Co., Ltd.
g. Yoshio Komatsu
i. Cutting sheet
j. Kobayashi kogeisha Co., Ltd.

a. 藤井毛織ビル モニュメント "地球樹"
b. 大阪府大阪市
c. 藤井毛織
d. 篠宮秀夫／鞠子隆／プロデューサー＝坂根進／アートディレクター＝富田隆博
e. 児島正剛／プロダクトマネージャー＝木戸康人／プロモーター＝浜上晴市, 中山隆／エンジニア＝折笠智和, 鈴木俊幸
f. 乃村工藝社
g. 大東正巳
h. 企業ビルが建ち並ぶ大阪備後町の一角，藤井毛織ビルの公開空地に完成した "地球樹" は，藤井毛織ビルの竣工を記念する屋外モニュメントである．備後町地域のもつ冷たく殺風景な雰囲気を，潤いのある人間性豊かな空間に創り変えることを強く意図し，環境オブジェと呼ぶにふさわしい造形の創出を目指したものである．"地球樹" はホワイトブロンズの枝をステンレスの葉で覆い，内部は中空，球状の外観を程している．ステンレスの葉には，地球上の陸と海を表す鏡面とナシ地2種類の仕上げがなされ，企業のもつ国際性がシンボリックに示されるとともに球体のもつ柔らかな造形感の表出が図られている．また "地球樹" の内部には，都市環境の守護神にも喩うべき "黄金の小鳥" が枝にとまり，定時に囀り，時を告げる．歩いてここを通り過ぎる人のなかには，この "黄金の小鳥" を発見し，驚嘆の歓声をあげ指をさすシーンも見られるにちがいない．また夜には，床面及び樹の内部にセットされた照明が灯り，四季の装いをかえて輝く，特に "地球樹" の内部空間は，夜の照明演出のために生かされ，あたかも巨大な "ぼんぼり" であるかのように周辺に心地よい幻想的な光を放つ．またクリスマスのシーズンには，きらきら光るチボリライトで埋められ，ここにまた季節感を映し出す新たな環境が現出する――など，四季の装いをかえて輝く "地球樹" のモニュメントは，大阪備後町周域の都市空間に溶け込み，新しいランドマーク的な役割を果たすものと確信する．
i. 葉＝ステンレス（鏡面・ツヤ消し）／樹（円柱）＝ステンレス鏡面／枝＝ホワイトブロンズ鋳物
j. 乃村工藝社

a. "GROBE TREE"
b. Osaka-shi, Osaka
c. Fujii Keori Co., Ltd.
d. Susumu Sakane, Takahiro Tomita, Hideo Shinomiya, Takashi Mariko
e. Masatake Kojima, Yasuto Kido, Seiichi Hamagami, Takashi Nakayama, Tomokazu Origasa, Toshiyuki Suzuki
f. Nomura Display Co., Ltd.
g. Masami Daito
h. The "Globe tree", which has been completed in the open vecant lot of Fujii Keori Building at the corner of Bingocho, Osaka City where buildings of enterprises stand in row, is an outdoor monument in commemoration of the completion of the Fujii Keori Building, The concept aims at creating a formative arts worthy of what is called as an environmental objet by a determined attempt at reconstructing the cold, rough atmosphere of the Bingo-cho area, into a tasteful, humanistically affluent space. The "Globe tree" presents a spherical external appearance, hollow inside, with the branches made of white bronze covered by the leaves made of stainless steel. On the surface of the stainless leaves are processed by the two kinds of finishes, mirror finish and matte finish each expressing the land and the sea, respectively. This symbolically indicates the internationalism that enterprises have as well as the intention of expressing the sense of soft formative arts that the spherical body possesses. Inside, the "Globe tree", a "Golden bird" comparable to the guardian god of the town environment perches on a twig, chiming the hours. It is most likely that scenes be seen in the future where some of the passersby in this street, noticing this "Golden bird", will point the bird with vociferous cheers is open-eyed wonder. At night, on the other hand, the illuminations, set on the floor and inside the tree, come on and blaze in the garb which is changed every season. The internal space of the "Globe tree", in particular, is utilized for night illumination presentation, emitting a pleasant, fantastic light all over around as if it were a huge paper-coverd lamp stand. In the christmastime, the tree is covered with tivoli lights, producing a new environment which reflects here again a sense of the season. It is our firm conviction that the monument of this glistening "Globe tree" with its dress changed every season, integrating itself into the urban space of Bingo-cho of Osaka City, will play a new landmark-like role.
i. Leaf: Stainless steel (mirror finish / matte finish); Tree (pillar): Stainless steel mirror finish; Branch: White bronze
j. Nomura Display Co., Ltd.

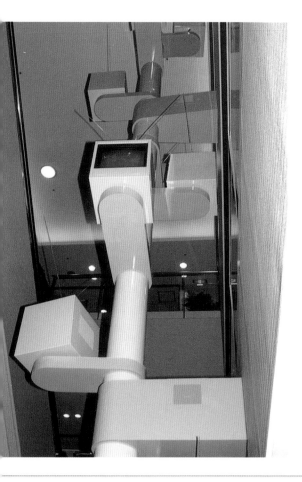

a. ポポロ「モニュメント」
b. 広島県呉市
c. CVB ポポロ
d. 大昌工芸開発センター
e. 竹内浩一／井下元
f. 大昌工芸
g. ギンレイフォト
h. モニュメンタルで，ボリュームのある"映像ツリー"を表現．視覚的に，ホットな感覚がねらい．
i. ボンデ鋼板（スチール）
j. 大昌工芸

a. POPOLO "MONUMENT"
b. Kure-shi, Hiroshima
c. CVB Poporo Co., Ltd.
d. Taisho Kogei Co., Ltd. ; Design Development Center
e. Koichi Takeuchi, Hazime Inoshita
f. Taisho Kogei Co., Ltd.
g. Ginrei Photo
h. An expression of a "Video Tree" that is both monumental and voluminous. The concept is an attempt at presenting a sense of excitement in hte heart of the city.
i. Bonderized steel plate
j. Taisho Kogei Co., Ltd.

---

a. 日本キリスト改革派 東京恩寵教会
b. 東京都渋谷区
c. 日本キリスト改革派 東京恩寵教会
d. 野老正昭
e. 野老正昭
f. 清水建設
g. 畑亮夫

h. 都心部に建つプロテスタントの教会堂の採光用ハイサイドライトの調光装置を利用したシンボル．
i. ステンレス／アルミ
j. 野老設計事務所

a. TOKYO ONCHO REFORMED CHURCH
b. Shibuya-ku, Tokyo
c. Tokyo Oncho Reformed Church
d. Masaaki Tokoro
e. Masaaki Tokoro
f. Shimizu Construction Co., Ltd.
g. Ryo Hata

h. A symbol that utilizes the light adjustment device of the high sidelight for lighting in a protestant church standing in hte heart of the city.
i. Stainless steel / Aluminum
j. Tokoro Planning Office

a. 広島 MID ビル
b. 広島県広島市
c. 松下興産
d. 出江寛建築事務所
e. 出江寛建築事務所（出江寛）
f. 清水建設・フジタ工業・大林組共同企業体
g. スタジオ・村井（村井修）
h. 主たる建築の裏通りはなおざりに成りやすい．建物にスーパーグラフィックを描いて裏通りに華を添えた．
i. 複合石綿板35ビニールペンキ塗装仕上げ
j. 出江寛建築事務所

a. HIROSHIMA MID BUILDING
b. Hiroshima-shi, Hiroshima
c. Matsushita Kosan
d. Kan Izue Architect & Associates
e. Kan Izue Architect & Associates / Kan Izue
f. Shimizu Construction Co., Ltd.; Fujita Corporation; Ohbayashi-Gumi, Ltd.　J.V.
g. Studio-Murai (Osamu Murai)
h. The back street of the main building tends to be neglected. Drawing a super graphic picture on the building adds color to the back street.
i. Composite asbestos plate (a) 35 / Vinyl paint coating finish
j. Kan Izue Architect & Associates

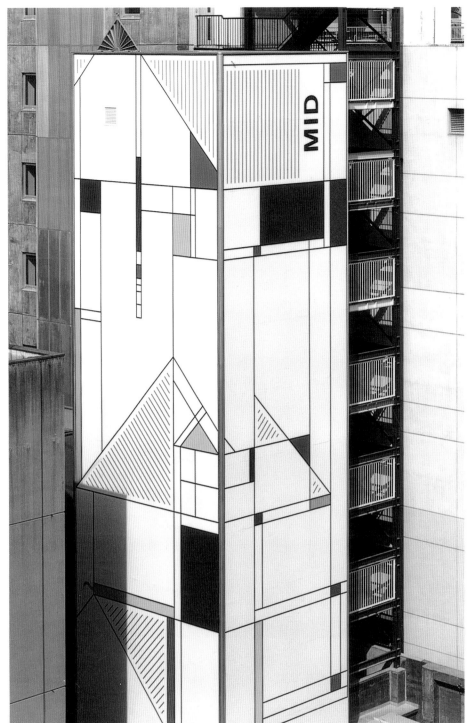

a. 日本橋人形町ショッピングモール
b. 東京都中央区
c. 人形町商店街／東京都中央区
d. 三枝公一
e. 佐藤康／赤間茂／村越雅行
f. コトブキ
g. 佐藤康
h. 「トラディショナルタウン」として，古きよき歴史の中に新しい表情が見え隠れし，楽しいイメージをもったショッピングモールを提案したものである．
i. 花崗岩（白御影・赤御影）／アルミ鋳物／アルミ合金押出型材／銅板／ボンデ鋼板
j. サエグサ・都市・建築設計事務所

a. NIHONBASHI NINGYOCHO SHOPPING MALL
b. Chuo-ku, Tokyo
c. Ningyocho shopping street cooperation / Tokyo Chuo-ward office engineering Dept.
d. Koichi Saegusa
e. Yasushi Sato, Shigeru Akama, Masayuki Murakoshi
f. Kotobuki Seating Co., Ltd.
g. Yasushi Sato
h. A suggestion of a shopping mall with a pleasant image where a new expression becomes now sensible and now insensible, in the history of good old days of the "Traditional Town".
i. Granite (white granite / Red granite) / Aluminum casting / Aluminum alloy extruded profile / Copper plate / Bonderized steel plate
j. Saegusa Urban & Architects Design office

a. 元町ショッピングモール
b. 神奈川県横浜市
c. 元町 SS 会
d. 後藤田茂樹
e. デザイン計画＝金子恒雄／サイン＝豊口協／モニュメント＝箕原正
f. 大成建設
g. 大成建設
h. 元町の求める本物志向から自然石を用い，ボンエルフ型のユニークな道空間を創出した．
i. 御影石（ポルトガル産，韓国産）／御影ピンコロ石／御影質タイル
j. 大成建設設計本部

a. MOTOMACHI SHOPPING MALL IN YOKOHAMA
b. Yokohama-shi, Kanagawa
c. Motomachi Shopping Street Association
d. Shigeki Gotoda
e. Design : Tsuneo Kaneko, Kyo Toyoguchi ; Monument : Tadashi Minohara
f. Taisei Corporation
g. Taesei Corporation
h. A creation of a unique street space of a Bon-elfe type by using natural stone to meet the genuine-article-oriented requirement of Motomachi.
i. Granite (from Portugal and Korea) / Mikage small size stone / Granite qualty tile
j. Taisei Corporation

a. バスシェルター千葉
b. 千葉県千葉市
c. 千葉県バス協会
d. 村井信夫
e. デンコー設計部
f. デンコー設計部
h. 市役所前のバス停は乗降客の憩いの場でもある．バック
　の森と建物と調和する和風調でまとめた．
i. ステンレス／スチール／ポリカーボネート
j. デンコー

a. BUS STOP AWNING
b. Chiba-shi, Chiba
c. Chiba Bus Association
d. Nobuo Murai
e. Denko Co., Ltd.
f. Denko Co., Ltd.
h. The bus stop in front of the City Office is a place for
　repose, as well. The concept attempts to arranges the
　design of the station in Japanese style to reconcile it
　with the back ground of the wood and buildings.
i. Stainless steel / Steel / Polycarbonate
j. Denko Co., Ltd.

a. バスターミナルシェルター江戸川
b. 東京都江戸川区
c. 東京都交通局
d. 村井信夫
e. デンコー設計部
f. デンコー
i. スチール／ステンレス／ポリカーボネート／網入ガラス
j. デンコー

a. BUS STATION
b. Edogawa-ku, Tokyo
c. Traffic Bureau of Tokyo
d. Nobuo Murai
e. Denko Co., Ltd.
f. Denko Co., Ltd.
i. Steel / Stainless Steel / Polycarbonate / Wired glass
j. Denko Co., Ltd.

a. バスシェルター横浜
b. 神奈川県横浜市
c. 東京急行電鉄
d. 村井信夫
e. デンコー設計部
f. デンコー
i. ポリカーボネート／スチール
j. デンコー

a. BUS STOP
b. Yokohama-shi, Kanagawa
c. Tokyo Kyuko Dentetsu Co., Ltd.
d. Nobuo Murai
e. Denko Co., Ltd.
f. Denko Co., Ltd.
i. Polycarbonate / Steel
j. Denko Co., Ltd.

a. バスターミナルシェルター川崎
b. 神奈川県川崎市
c. 川崎市土木局
d. 都市環境研究所
e. 都市環境研究所
f. デンコー
i. ステンレス／ポリカーボネート
j. デンコー

a. BUS STOP
b. Kawasaki-shi, Kanagawa
c. Kawasaki-shi, Office
d. Laboratory of Town Environmental
e. Laboratory of Town Environmental
f. Denko Co., Ltd.
i. Stainless steel / Polycarbonate
j. Denko Co., Ltd.

a. バスターミナルシェルター千代田
b. 東京都千代田区
c. 東京都交通局
d. 岡田誠之助
e. デンコー設計部
f. デンコー
i. アルミ／スチール
j. デンコー

a. AWNING FOR BUS STATION
b. Chiyoda-ku, Tokyo
c. Traffic Bureau of Tokyo
d. Seinosuke Okada
e. Denko Co., Ltd.
f. Denko Co., Ltd.
i. Aluminum / Steel
j. Denko Co., Ltd.

a. エレファント
b. 北海道札幌市
c. 北海道中央バス
d. 村井信夫
e. デンコー設計部
f. デンコー札幌営業所
h. 耐候性と保温性を重視. 路線の環境とマッチするようデ
　ザイン. バス待合所の未来を提案.
i. GRC／アルミサッシ／ポリカーボネート
j. デンコー

a. BUS STOP MODEL "ELEPHANT"
b. Sapporo-shi, Hokkaido
c. Hokkaido Chuo Bus Co., Ltd.
d. Nobuo Murai
e. Denko Co., Ltd.
f. Denko Co., Ltd.
h. Emphasis is laid on weather proof and heat retaining
　property. The concept is an attempt at designing the
　bus stop so that it matches the environment of the bus
　line. Our intention lies in proposing a future bus stop.
i. GRC / Aluminum sash / Polycarbonate
j. Denko Co., Ltd.

a. 自転車置場 A
b. 富山県下新川郡
c. 建設省富山工事事務所
d. デンコー北陸営業所
f. デンコー北陸営業所
h. 家からバス停までは自転車．それから先はバス．過密化する交通手段の解消を目指す設計である．
i. アルミ／スチール／セメント
j. デンコー

a. CYCLE PARK A
b. Shimoniikawa-gun, Toyama
c. Ministry of Construction, Toyama Office
d. Denko Co., Ltd.
f. Denko Co., Ltd.
h. Cycle riding from the house to the bus stop. Taking a bus for further trip. The design aims at solving the troubles arising from the over congestion in traffic means.
i. Aluminum / Steel / Cement
j. Denko Co., Ltd.

a. 自転車駐車場 A
b. 神奈川県平塚市
c. 平塚市役所
d. 創造社
e. 創造社
f. デンコー工事部
h. 学校の一部敷地を有効利用した二階建立体駐車場．
i. アルミ／スチール
j. デンコー

a. CYCLE PARK A
b. Hiratsuka-shi, Kanagawa
c. Hiratsuka City Office
d. Sozosha Co., Ltd.
e. Sozosha Co., Ltd.
f. Denko Co., Ltd.
h. A two-storied, solid cycle-park built by the efficient use of part of the campus site. The Accommodations for cycles.
i. Aluminum / Steel
j. Denko Co., Ltd.

a. 自転車駐車場 B
b. 静岡県新居町
c. 日本自転車普及協会
d. 杉原設計事務所
e. 杉原設計事務所
f. デンコー工事部
h. 日本自転車普及協会が全国に設置している理想的な大型自転車駐車場のひとつ．
i. スチール／カラー鉄板／コンクリート
j. デンコー

a. CYCLE PARK B
b. Arai-cho, Shizuoka
c. Japan Cycle Popularization Association
d. Architecture Sugihara
e. Architecture Sugihara
f. Denko Co., Ltd.
h. One of the ideal large size cycle parks installed all over the country by Japan Cycle Popularization Association. The reputation of the users is favorable.
i. Steel / Color steel plate / Concrete
j. Denko Co., Ltd.

a. 自転車置場 D
b. 東京都品川区
c. 勤労者住宅供給公社
d. 浅沼組
f. デンコー工事部
h. マンモス団地の自転車置場．主婦や子供たちにも利用しやすいよう入口をたっぷり取った設計．
i. アルミ／スチール／セメント／鉄筋
j. デンコー

a. CYCLE PARK D
b. Shinagawa-ku, Tokyo
c. Bureau of Labors Housing
d. Asanumagumi Co., Ltd.
f. Denko Co., Ltd.
h. A cycle park of a huge housing development. To provide easy use of this cycle park even for women and children, an entrance allowing an ample latitude has been designed.
i. Aluminum / Steel / Cement / Reinforcement bar
j. Denko Co., Ltd.

a. 自転車置場 E
b. 埼玉県狭山市
c. 狭山市役所
d. 清水建設
f. デンコー工事部
h. 市役所内の環境デザインにマッチするデザインであるとともに，利用しやすい場所に設置された．
i. アルミ／ステンレス／スチール／フッ素樹脂鋼板
j. デンコー

a. CYCLE PARK E
b. Sayama-shi, Saitama
c. Sayama City Office
d. Shimizu Construction Co., Ltd.
f. Denko Co., Ltd.
h. The cycle park is not only designed to match the environmental design around the City Office but also installed at a convenient place for use.
i. Aluminum / Stainless steel / Steel / Fluorine resin coated steel plate
j. Denko Co., Ltd.

a. 自転車置場 B
b. 新潟県長岡市
c. 建設省長岡工事事務所
f. デンコー北陸営業所
h. バス待合所に隣接し設置した自転車駐車場（バス・ロード・ステーション）．
i. アルミ／スチール
j. デンコー

a. CYCLE PARK B
b. Nagaoka-shi, Niigata
c. Ministry of Construction, Nagaoka Office
f. Denko Co., Ltd.
h. A cycle park installed adjacent to the bus stop (bus, road, and station). An ideal traffic means.
i. Aluminum / Steel
j. Denko Co., Ltd.

a. 自転車置場 C
b. 新潟県坂井町
c. 建設省北陸地方建設局長岡国道工事事務所
f. デンコー北陸営業所
i. アルミ／スチール／ポリカーボネート
j. デンコー

a. CYCLE PARK C
b. Sakai-cho, Niigata
c. Ministry of Construction, Nagaoka Office
f. Denko Co., Ltd.
i. Aluminum / Steel / Polycarbonate
j. Denko Co., Ltd.

a. 自転車置台（ラック）
d. 村井信夫
e. デンコー設計部
h. 自転車を効率的に収容するだけでなく，預ける人の気持ちになって，色，形状を工夫したデザイン.
i. スチール／ステンレス／アルミ
j. デンコー

a. CYCLE RAC FOR PARKING
d. Nobuo Murai
e. Denko Co., Ltd.
h. A design which not only has been made to efficiently accommodate cycles but also has been contrived in terms of color and shape by taking into consideration the state of user's mind.
i. Steel / Stainless steel / Aluminum
j. Denko Co., Ltd.

a. バス総合案内システム
b. 千葉県千葉市
c. 千葉県バス協会
d. 千葉県バス協会／デンコー
e. デンコー設計部
f. デンコー
h. バスを利用しやすくするためにコンピュータによる運行情報をコントロールする案内システム.
i. ステンレス／アルミ／アルポリック／強化ガラス／アクリル／ポリカーボネート
j. デンコー

a. INFORMATION SYSTEM OF BUS TRAFFIC
b. Chiba-shi, Chiba
c. Chiba Bus Association
d. Chiba Bus Association ; Denko Co., Ltd.
e. Denko Co., Ltd.
f. Denko Co., Ltd.
h. A guiding system in which bus operation information is controlled by a computer unit for the improvement of the availability of buses.
i. Stainless steel / Aluminum / Alpolic / Tempered glass / Acryl / Polycarbonate
j. Denko Co., Ltd.

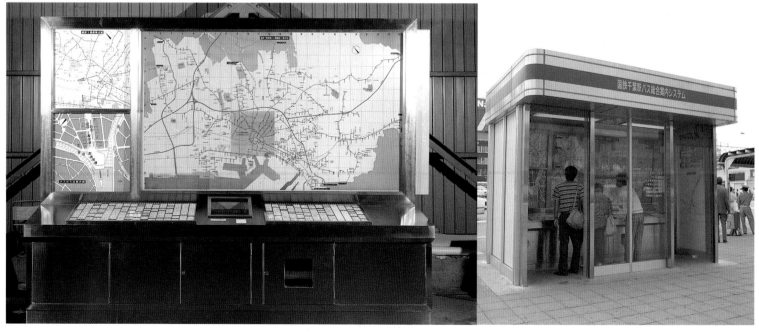

a. DK ポート
b. 新潟県
c. 新潟交通
d. 岡田誠之助
e. デンコー設計部
f. デンコー北陸営業所
i. アルミ／ポリカーボネート／プラメタル
j. デンコー

a. BUS STOP MODEL "DK PORT"
b. Niigata
c. Niigata Kotsu Co., Ltd.
d. Seinosuke Okada
e. Denko Co., Ltd.
f. Denko Co., Ltd.
i. Aluminum / Polycarbonate / Plastic metal
j. Denko Co., Ltd.

a. 電照式標識 A
b. 神奈川県川崎市
c. 川崎市土木局
d. 都市環境研究所
e. 都市環境研究所
f. デンコー
i. ステンレス／ポリカーボネート
j. デンコー

a. ILLUMINATED SIGN FOR BUS STOP A
b. Kawasaki-shi, Kanagawa
c. Kawasaki City Office
d. Laboratory of City Environmental
e. Laboratory of City Environmental
f. Denko Co., Ltd.
i. Stainless steel / Polycarbonate
j. Denko Co., Ltd.

a. 電照式標識 B
b. 神奈川県川崎市
c. 川崎地下街建設共同企業体
d. 日建設計
e. 日建設計
f. デンコー
i. ステンレス／ポリカーボネート／スチール強化ガラス／アクリル
j. デンコー

a. ILLUMINATED SIGN FOR BUS STOP B
b. Kawasaki-shi, Kanagawa
c. Trust of Kawasaki Basement
d. Nikken Design Co., Ltd.
e. Nikken Design Co., Ltd.
f. Denko Co., Ltd.
i. Stainless steel / Polycarbonate / Steel / Tempered glass / Acryl
j. Denko Co., Ltd.

a. バスシステム案内板
b. 東京都大田区
c. 京浜急行電鉄
d. デンコー企画部
e. デンコー企画部
f. デンコー工事部
h. 正確な地図をベースとした運行路線図は、どこで乗降したらよいかが事前によく分かる。
i. ステンレス／強化ガラス／アクリル
j. デンコー

a. SIGNBOARD FOR BUS STOP
b. Ota-ku, Tokyo
c. Keihin Kyuko Dentetsu Co., Ltd.
d. Denko Co., Ltd.
e. Denko Co., Ltd.
f. Denko Co., Ltd.
h. The operation route chart based on an accurate map acquires a good reputation because passengers can well understand in advance where to get on and off.
i. Stainless steel / Tempered glass / Acryl
j. Denko Co., Ltd.

a. 新交通システム案内板
b. 東京都目黒区
c. 東京急行電鉄
d. デンコー企画部
e. デンコー企画部
f. デンコー工事部
h. 路線図，時刻表，行先案内などバス利用に関する必要な情報をまとめて掲示する総合案内板．
i. ステンレス／スチール／強化ガラス／アクリル／アルポリック
j. デンコー

a. SIGNBOARD FOR BUS TRAFFIC
b. Meguro-ku, Tokyo
c. Tokyo Kyuko Dentetsu Co., Ltd.
d. Denko Co., Ltd.
e. Denko Co., Ltd.
f. Denko Co., Ltd.
h. A comprehensive information board that provides necessary information for the passengers who avail themselves of a bus, such as traffic route chart, time table, and destination information.
i. Stainless steel / Steel / Tempered glass / Acryl / Alpolic
j. Denko Co., Ltd.

a. 電照式標識
b. 神奈川県戸塚市
c. 神奈川中央交通
d. デンコー企画部
e. 高橋志保彦建築設計事務所
f. デンコー工事部
h. 東海道五十三次の宿場でもあった戸塚の街並の雰囲気を出すため切妻タイプのデザインとした．
i. ステンレス／ポリカーボネート／スチール／アクリル
j. デンコー

a. ILLUMINATED SIGN FOR BUS STOP
b. Totsuka-shi, Kanagawa
c. Kanagawa Chuo Kotsu Co., Ltd.
d. Denko Co., Ltd.
e. Architecture Shihohiko Takahashi
f. Denko Co., Ltd.
h. The sign has been designed on a gable style to produce an atmosphere of the rows of shops and houses on the streets of Totsuka City which once was one of the post towns of the old time fifty-three stages on the Tokaido highway.
i. Stainless steel / Polycarbonate / Steel / Acryl
j. Denko Co., Ltd.

a. 外照式案内板
b. 東京都大田区
c. 東京急行電鉄
d. デンコー企画部
e. デンコー企画部
f. デンコー工事部
h. 夜間も見やすく分かりやすい外照式案内板．同時にバス停が遠くからも識別できるよう工夫した．
i. ステンレス／強化ガラス／カイダック／アクリル
j. デンコー

a. ILLUMINATED SIGN FOR BUS TRAFFIC
b. Ota-ku, Tokyo
c. Tokyo Kyuko Dentetsu Co., Ltd.
d. Denko Co., Ltd.
e. Denko Co., Ltd.
f. Denko Co., Ltd.
h. A sign board of a exterior-illuminated type that is easy to read and understand even at night. A contrivance has been so made that a bus stop can be recognized from a distance.
i. Stainless steel / Tempered glass / Acryl
j. Denko Co., Ltd.

a. しらゆりⅠ型
b. 東京都中央区
c. はとバス
d. 岡田誠之助
e. 岡田誠之助
f. デンコー工事部
h. 二面式標識．
i. アルミ／ポリカーボネート／カイダック
j. デンコー

a. BUS STOP MODEL "SHIRAYURI I"
b. Chuo-ku, Tokyo
c. Hato Bus Co., Ltd.
d. Seinosuke Okada
e. Seinosuke Okada
f. Denko Co., Ltd.
h. Double-surface type sign board.
i. Aluminum / Polycarbonate /
j. Denko Co., Ltd.

a. 新交通システム用電照式標識
b. 東京都世田谷区
c. 東京急行電鉄
d. デンコー企画部
e. デンコー企画部
f. デンコー
h. 次のバス発車時刻がわかる，市民の足として，それまでの時間を有効につかえるよう工夫した．
i. ステンレス／ポリカーボネート／強化ガラス／鉄骨
j. デンコー

a. ILLUMINATED SIGN FOR TRAFFIC
b. Setagaya-ku, Tokyo
c. Tokyo Kyuko Dentetsu Co., Ltd.
d. Denko Co., Ltd.
e. Denko Co., Ltd.
f. Denko Co., Ltd.
h. The sign has been so designed as to allow the passengers to make effective use of the waiting time until the next bus by notifying them the next departure time.
i. Stainless steel / Polycarbonate / Tempered glass / Steel frame
j. Denko Co., Ltd.

a. 内照式案内板
b. 神奈川県川崎市
c. 川崎市土木局
d. 都市環境研究所
e. 都市環境研究所
f. デンコー工事部
i. ステンレス／スチール／強化ガラス／銅板アルポリック
j. デンコー

a. ILLUMINATED SIGN FOR BUS TRAFFIC
b. Kawasaki-shi, Kanagawa
c. Kawasaki City Office
d. Laboratory of City Environmental
e. Laboratory of City Environmental
f. Denko Co., Ltd.
i. Stainless steel / Steel / Tempered glass / Copper plat / Alpolic
j. Denko Co., Ltd.

a. 横浜新都市ビル（横浜そごう）
b. 神奈川県横浜市
c. 横浜新都市センター／横浜スカイビル
d. 三菱地所第二建築部／石本建築事務所
e. 三菱地所第二建築部（大国道夫, 大沢秀雄）／メックデザインインターナショナル／乃村工藝社／丹青社
f. メックデザインインターナショナル／乃村工藝社／丹青社
g. 三輪晃久写真研究所／ジャプロ／日本グラフィック
h. 回遊性のあるペデストリアンデッキに次々と展開するモニュメント・ファニチャー群.
i. 方位盤＝花崗岩, ステンレス／風のオブジェ＝ステンレスロッド
j. 三菱地所

a. YOKOHAMA SHINTOSHI BUILDING
b. Yokohama-shi, Kanagawa
c. Yokohama shintoshi Center Co., Ltd.; Yokohama Sky Building Co., Ltd.
d. Mitsubishi Estate Co.,Ltd. /Ishimoto Architectural Office
e. Mitsubishi Estate Co., Ltd.: Michio Okuni, Hideo Osawa, MEC Design International Corporation / Nomura Display; Tanseisha
f. MEC Design International Corporation; Nomura Display; Tanseisha
g. Kohkyu Miwa Architectural Photograph Laboratory; JAPRO, Nihon Graphic
h. One group of monuments and furniture which develop one after another as the visitors walk on the pedestrian deck which invite them to a circular trip.
i. Direction indicator / Granite / Stainless steel / Wind objet / Stainless steel rod
j. Mitsubishi Estate Co., Ltd.

a. 甲府市朝日町ストリートファニチャー
b. 山梨県甲府市
c. 山梨県甲府市土木事務所
d. 杉山晃一
e. 星明臣／多田和典
f. 吉沢建設
g. 古賀修
h. 街路灯・電柱・照明付駒止・灰皿付くず箱・ベンチの
　5点を全て耐候性剛材を使用し加工した.
i. 耐候性剛材／パーカライジング加工
j. ヤシマ

a. KOFU-SHI ASAHI-CHO STREET FURNITURE
b. Kofu shi, Yamanashi
d. Koichi Sugiyama
e. Akiomi Hoshi, Kazunori Tada
f. Yoshizawa Kensetsu Co., Ltd.
g. Osamu Koga
h. Weather proof high strength material has been used for
   and fabricated into all of the five components, i.e.,
   outdoor lightings, electric poles, guardrails with lights,
   trash baskets with ash trays, and benches.
i. Weatherproof high strength steel / Parkarizing process-
   ing
j. Yashima Co., Ltd.

a. お天気情報板
b. 愛知県名古屋市
c. 広小路名駅商店街
d. 松本義隆
e. 設計企画＝樋尾賢吾
f. 日本街路灯製造
g. 加藤政雄
h. NTT電話BOXの上にメロディー付時計及びお天気総
　合情報板を取り付けたユニークなモニュメント.
i. ステンレス SUS304
j. 日本街路灯製造

a. WEATHER MONUMENT
b. Nagoya-shi, Aichi
c. Hirokoji-Meieki Shotengai
d. Yoshitaka Matsumoto
e. Planning : Kengo Hio
f. Japan Outdoor Lighting Co., Ltd.
g. Masao Kato
h. A unique monument provided with a NTT telephone box
   on which a melody clock and a general weather bulletin
   board are installed.
i. Stainless steel
j. Japan Outdoor Lighting Co., Ltd.

a. モニュメント街路灯及び脚灯
b. 石川県金沢市
c. 堅町商店街
d. 水辺博
e. 企画＝黒川淳子／設計＝樋尾賢吾
f. 日本街路灯製造
g. 加藤政雄
i. SUS304／脚灯＝鋳物焼付塗装／灯具＝400Wリフレ
　クターランプ
j. 日本街路灯製造

a. MONUMENT OUTDOOR LIGHTING & FOOT
LIGHTING
b. Kanazawa-shi, Ishikawa
c. Tatemachi-shotengai
d. Hiroshi Mizube
e. Atsuko Kurokawa, Kengo Hio
f. Japan Outdoor Lighting Co., Ltd.
g. Masao Kato
i. SUS 304 ; Foot lamp : Baking paint on casting ; lamp
fixtures : 400 W reflector lamp ; Foot lamp : three-lights
13 Watt each
j. Japan Outdoor Lighting Co., Ltd.

a. 電話ボックス
b. 東京都練馬区
c. 西友
d. 田中一光
e. スーパーポテト
f. 小林工芸社
g. 小松好雄
i. 鋼板／ガラス／ナラ材
j. 小林工芸社

a. TELEPHONE BOX
b. Nerima-ku, Tokyo
c. Seiyu Co., Ltd.
d. Ikko Tanaka
e. Super Potato
f. Kobayashi Kogeisha Co., Ltd.
g. Yoshio Komatsu
i. Steel plate / Glass / Japanese oakwood
j. Kobayashi Kogeisha Co., Ltd.

a. トランスパッケージ「ベンチ」
b. 広島県広島市
c. 中国電力配電部
d. 大昌工芸環境デザイン研究所
e. 小池晋弘／井上峯雄
f. 大昌工芸
g. 小池晋弘
h. トランスを地上に降ろす事により、電柱の煩雑さを解消、
　その化粧化をベンチ式として「レスト・スペース」とした。
i. FRP
j. 大昌工芸

a. TRANSPACKAGE "BENCH"
b. Hiroshima-shi, Hiroshima
c. Chugoku Electric Power Inc., Power Distribution Department
d. Taisho Kogei Co., Ltd. ; Environmental Design Institute
e. Nobuhiro Koike, Mineo Inoue
f. Taisho Kogei Co., Ltd.
g. Nobuhiro Koike
h. Bringing down the transformers on the ground has
solved the nuisance of the existence of poles. For
dressing of the transformers, they are made into a
bench-type "Rest space".
i. FRP
j. Taisho Kogei Co., Ltd.

a. 江戸川区環境サイン計画
b. 東京都江戸川区
c. 江戸川区役所総務部　環境促進事業団
d. スペース・デザイン・ハッピー：石井敏和
e. 泉沢誠志，大越圭子
f. 東芸社
g. 石井敏和

h. やすらぎとうるおいのある都市空間，住み心地よい街，都市景観を考慮した環境サインを試みた。
i. スチール焼付／ステンレス鏡面／ネオン管／スリーエムカラーフィルム／アクリル
j. スペース・デザイン・ハッピー

a. EDOGAWA WARD OFFICE ENVIRONMENTAL
　 SIGN PLAN
b. Edogawa-ku, Tokyo
c. Edogawa Ward office
d. Space Design Happy : Toshikazu Ishii
e. Seishi Izumizawa, Keiko Okoshi
f. Togeisha Co., Ltd.
g. Toshikazu Ishii

h. The concept is an attempt at presenting an environmental sign which takes into consideration an urban landscape that will provide an urban space with repose and charm and will make the city comfortable to live in.
i. Baking paint on Steel / Stainless steel mirror finish / Neon tube / 3-M color film / Acryl
j. Space Design Happy

a. おもいはせの路（玉川左岸）サイン
b. 東京都世田谷区
c. 世田谷区土木部工事第二課
d. 世田谷区企画部都市デザイン室
e. AUR（長島孝一／山路清貴／秋元馨）
f. 光和工業
g. AUR（秋元馨）
h. 散策路周辺地区の歴史性と景観に関連した素材とモチーフによりデザインを展開している.

i. 大谷石／芦野石／丹銅板／スクラッチタイル
j. AUR 建築・都市・研究コンサルタント

a. "OMOIHASE-NO-MICHI" SIGN
b. Setagaya-ku, Tokyo
c. Setagaya Ward, Civil Engineering Division
d. Setagaya Ward, Urban Design Section, Planning Division
e. AUR Architectural Urban Design Research Consultants Co., Ltd. : Koichi Nagashima, Kiyotaka Yamaji, Kaoru Akimoto
f. Kowa Kogyo Co., Ltd.

g. AUR Architectural Urban Design Research Consultants Co., Ltd. : Kaoru Akimoto
h. The design develops on the bassis of the historical background of the peripheral region of the walkway and the materials associated with the landscape.
i. Oya stone / Ashino stone / Red copper plate / Scratched tile
j. AUR Architectural Urban Design Research Consultants Co., Ltd.

a. 長崎バイオパークサイン計画
b. 長崎県西彼杵郡
c. 長崎バイオパーク
d. テイ・グラバー
e. テイ・グラバー／日本設計事務所／日本国土開発
f. テイ・グラバー
g. テイ・グラバー
h. 動，植物公園における最小限の情報をサインにまとめ
た．名称，分布，生態，食物等．
i. アルミ板／スコッチカルシート／アクリル板／シルク印刷
j. テイ・グラバー

a. DESIGN TO SIGN FOR NAGASAKI BIO PARK
b. Nishisonogi-gun, Nagasaki
c. Nagasaki Bio Park Co., Ltd.
d. T. Glover Co., Ltd.
e. T. Glover Co., Ltd. / Nihon Architects Engineers &
Consultants, Inc. / JDC Corporation
f. T. Glover Co., Ltd.
g. T. Glover Co., Ltd.
h. A minimum of information on the zoo and botanical
garden, such as nomenclature, distribution, ecology,
feed, and the like has been summarized in the sign.
i. Aluminum plate / Scotch calsheet / Acryl plate / Silk
printing
j. T. Glover Co., Ltd.

a. 大和ライフ本社サインシステム
b. 京都府京都市
c. 大和ライフ
d. 中村政慶
e. 迫田昌治
f. 清水建設／サイン＝美術宣伝社
g. フジタ写真工房／迫田昌治
h. ビルデザインと企業のサインとの一体化を図ることにより，新たなCIを生み出している。
i. ステンレス鏡面仕上／アクリル板／鋼板焼付塗装／外壁＝ミラーガラス
j. 中村建築設計事務所

a. DAIWA LIFE CO., LTD. HEAD OFFICE SIGN SYSTEM
b. Kyoto-shi, Kyoto
c. Daiwa Life Co., Ltd.
d. Masayoshi Nakamura
e. Masaharu Sakoda
f. Shimizu Construction Co., Ltd., ; Bijutsu Senden-sha
g. Fujita Photo Studio, Masaharu Sakoda
h. The attempt at integrating the building design and the sign of the enterprise creates a new corporate identity.
i. Stainless steel mirror finish / Acryl plate / Baking paint on Steel ; External wall : Mirror glass
j. Nakamura Architectural Planning Office

a. イーストランド
b. 岡山県津山市
c. 三和
d. 神尾勝宏
f. デンショク
g. 福本正明

h. 先端情報の発信地としての鋭角的感覚，力強さと人々に信頼されるSCづくりへの願いをこめて．
j. 船場SC綜合開発研究所

a. EAST LAND
b. Tsuyama-shi, Okayama
c. Sanwa
d. Katsuhiro Kamio
f. Denshyoku
g. Masaaki Hukumoto

h. With all best wishes for creating an acute sense as the place of dispatching advanced technological information, strength, and SC on which people place enough reliability.
j. Semba Corporation

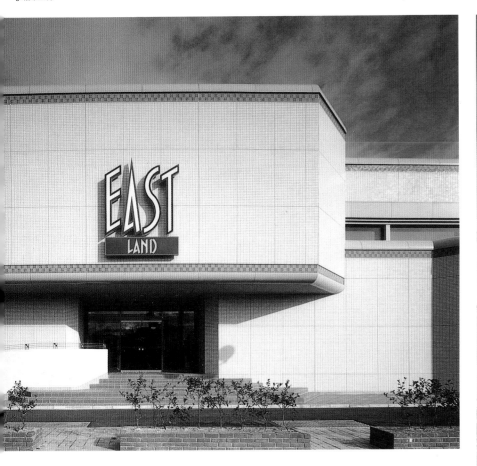

a. ヤマハ発動機第5工場サイン・色彩計画
b. 静岡県磐田市
c. ヤマハ発動機
d. 宮沢功／村井大三郎
e. 横田保生／岡本章伺
f. スズオカ／亜興／関西ペイント／日本ペイント

g. 梅田正明
h. 工場全体を物と人の入出力機と考え、物の動線を緑とし、人の動線を青とし、工場の環境づくりを行った.
i. ウレタン系床用塗材
j. GK グラフィックス

a. COLOR PLAN OF SIGNS IN No.5 PLNAT
b. Iwata-shi, Shizuoka
c. Yamaha Motor Co., Ltd.
d. Isao Miyazawa, Daizaburo Murai
e. Yasuo Yokota, Shoji Okamoto

f. Suzuoka Co., Ltd.; Ako Co., Ltd.; Kansai Paint Co., Ltd.; Nippon Paint Co., Ltd.
g. Masaaki Umeda

h. The scheme, assuming that the whole plant is an output / input device, attempts to create an environment of the plant where green and blue colors are used for the paths of flow of products and people, respectively.
i. Urethane-base paint for floor
j. GK Graphic Assocites

a. 横浜そごうサイン計画
b. 神奈川県横浜市
c. 横浜そごう
d. 番浦泰三
e. 東海林基文／永田雅一
f. アルス
g. アルス

h. 広大な百貨店のサイン計画として，ダイナミックにかつサイン機能を最優先させた．
i. スチールメラミン焼付／シルクプロセス印刷
j. アルス HED 事業部

a. YOKOHAMA SOGO SIGN PLANNING
b. Yokohama-shi, Kanagawa
c. Yokohama Sogo
d. Taizo Ban-ura
e. Motofumi Shoji, Masakazu Nagata
f. Arusu Co., Ltd.
g. Arusu Co., Ltd.

h. The scheme of making the sign of the huge department store intends to install a dynamic sign as giving priority over its function.
i. Baking melamine on Steel / Silk process printing
j. Arusu Co., Ltd.

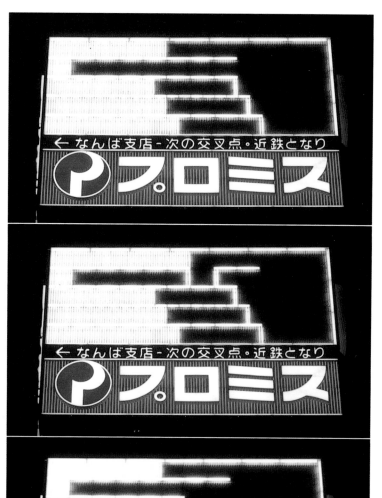

a. コットンクラブ
b. 新潟県三条市
c. コットンクラブ
d. 刈屋剛
e. 刈屋剛
f. アスカデザイン室
g. 刈屋剛
i. 真鍮
j. アスカデザイン室

a. COTTON CLUB
b. Sanjo-shi, Niigata
c. Cotton Club
d. Go Kariya
e. Go Kariya
f. Aska Inc.
g. Go Kariya
i. Brass
j. Aska Inc.

a. プロミス・サイン広告
b. 大阪府大阪市
c. プロミス
d. 小島龍三
e. 大黒昌子
f. 朝日電装
g. 西村出
h. 日本一ビッグな〈指示〉誘導ネオン，大阪道頓堀の情緒になじむ愉しい動きを意図．
i. 鉄骨／鉄板／ネオン
j. 小島ディレクターズ

a. PROMISE NEON SIGN
b. Osaka-shi, Osaka
c. Promise Co., Ltd.
d. Ryuzo Kojima
e. Masako Daikoku
f. Asahi Denso Co., Ltd.
g. Izuru Nishimura
h. One of the biggest 〈instruction〉 guidance neon sign in Japan. The concept is an attempt at presenting a pleasant movement in the sign that will adapt itself to the atmosphere of Osaka Dotonbori Street.
i. Steel frame / Steel plate / Neon
j. Kojima Directors

a. Boutique 花
b. 新潟県加茂市
c. Boutique 花
d. 刈屋剛
e. 刈屋剛
g. 刈屋剛
i. アクリル
j. アスカデザイン室

a. BOUTIQUE HANA
b. Kamo-shi, Niigata
c. Boutique Hana
d. Go Kariya
e. Go Kariya
g. Go Kariya
i. Acryl
j. Aska Inc.

a. 長崎オランダ村サイン計画
b. 長崎県西彼杵郡
c. 長崎オランダ村
d. テイ・グラバー
e. テイ・グラバー／日本設計事務所／日本国土開発
f. テイ・グラバー
g. テイ・グラバー
h. 17世紀オランダの街づくり，景観の一部としてサインの開発，形状，素材，ヴィジュアル等．
i. スチール／スコッチカルシート／シルク印刷
j. テイ・グラバー

a. DESIGN OF SIGN FOR NAGASAKI HOLLAND VILLAGE
b. Nishisonogi-gun, Nagasaki
c. Nagasaki Holland village Co., Ltd.
d. T. Glover Co., Ltd.
e. T. Glover Co., Ltd. / Nihon Architects Engineers & Consultants, Inc. / JDC Corporation
f. T. Glover Co., Ltd.
g. T. Glover Co., Ltd.
h. A construction of a Dutch town in the 17 Century. As part of its landscape, the sign has been developed in terms of shape, materials, visuality, and the like.
i. Steel / Scotch calsheet / Silk printing
j. T. Glover Co., Ltd.

a. サイン（光が丘西武店内サイン）
b. 東京都練馬区
c. 西友
d. 田中一光
e. 広村正章
f. 小林工芸社
g. 小松好雄
i. ステンレス／アクリル
j. 小林工芸社

a. HIKARIGAOKA SEIBU SIGNS
b. Nerima-ku, Tokyo
c. Seiyu Co., Ltd.
d. Ikko Tanaka
e. Masaaki Hiromura
f. Kobayashi Kogeisha Co., Ltd.
g. Yoshio Komatsu
i. Stainless steel / Acryl
j. Kobayashi Kogeisha Co., Ltd.

a. ブックスうかいや
b. 兵庫県姫路市
c. うかいや書店
d. 野村邦弘
e. 野村邦弘
f. のむら工芸
g. 今村幸廣
i. 主柱表面＝亜鉛鉄板焼付／広告面＝アクリル
j. のむら工芸

a. BOOKS UKAIYA
b. Himeji-shi, Hyogo
c. Ukaiya Shoten
d. Kunihiro Nomura
e. Kunihiro Nomura
f. Nomura Kougei
g. Yukihiro Imamura
i. Main pillar surface : Baking paint on galvanized steel
plate ; Advertising surface : Acryl
j. Nomura Kougei

a. グランドコーポ青山
b. 兵庫県姫路市
c. 青山開発
d. 野村邦弘
e. 野村邦弘
f. のむら工芸
g. 今村幸廣
i. 主柱面＝亜鉛鉄板焼付／広告面＝アクリル
j. のむら工芸

a. GRAND CORPO AOYAMA
b. Himeji-shi, Hyogo
c. Aoyama Kaihatsu Inc.
d. Kunihiro Nomura
e. Kunihiro Nomura
f. Nomura Kougei
g. Yukihiro Imamura
i. Main pillar surface : Baking paint on galvanized steel
plate ; Advertising surface : Acryl
j. Nomura Kougei

a. カフェ・クレイトンハウス
b. 兵庫県姫路市
c. カフェ・クレイトンハウス
d. 野村邦弘
e. 野村邦弘
f. のむら工芸
g. 今村幸廣
i. 看板面＝カラースパン／文字＝ピット文字
j. のむら工芸

a. CAFÉ CRAIGHTON HOUSE
b. Himeji-shi, Hyogo
c. Café Craighton House
d. Kunihiro Nomura
e. Kunihiro Nomura
f. Nomura Kougei
g. Yukihiro Imamura
i. Sign board surface : Color spandrel ; Character : Pit
character
j. Nomura Kougei

a. ガラスのサイン
b. 東京都町田市
c. 住宅・都市整備公団
e. 松岡二三夫／丸山幸子
g. 加藤清仁
h. ライト感覚な素材.
i. 強化ガラス／スチールフレーム／圧着シート
j. ベル環境計画事務所

a. SIGN OF GLASS
b. Machida-shi, Tokyo
c. Jyutaku Toshi Seibikodan
e. Fumio Matsuoka, Sachiko Maruyama
g. Kiyohito Kato
h. A material of a light sense.
i. Tempered glass / Steel frame / Clad sheet
j. Bel Landscape Architectural Design Office

a. 施設サイン
b. 沖縄県那覇市
c. 西友
d. 飯田修市
e. 飯田修市　宇野良子
f. 小林工芸社
g. 飯田修市
i. 鋼板／アクリル／ネオン
j. 小林工芸社

a. SHOP SIGN
b. Naha-shi, Okinawa
c. Seiyu Co., Ltd.
d. Shuichi Iida
e. Shuichi Iida
f. Kobayashi Kougeisha Co., Ltd.
g. Shuichi Iida
i. Steel plate / Acryl / Neon
j. Kobayashi Kougeisha Co., Ltd.

a. カフェ・グラスラビット
h. 兵庫県姫路市
c. カフェ・グラスラビット
d. 野村邦弘
e. 野村邦弘
f. のむら工芸
g. 今村幸廣
h. 欧風調の伝統的なスタイルをスチールパイプの組合せで表現.
i. 主柱:スチールパイプ加工／看板面:板装 OP 仕上
j. のむら工芸

a. CAFÉ GLASS RABBIT
b. Himeji-shi, Hyogo
c. Café Glass Rabbit
d. Kunihiro Nomura
e. Kunihiro Nomura
f. Nomura Kougei
g. Yukihiro Imamura
h. The combination of steel pipes is an attempt at expressing an European traditional style.
i. Main pillar : Steel pipe working ; Sign surface plate : OP finish
j. Nomura Kougei

a. カフェ・レストラン ドンキーパパ
b. 兵庫県姫路市
c. カフェ・レストラン ドンキーパパ
d. 野村邦弘
e. 野村邦弘
f. のむら工芸
g. 今村幸廣
i. フレーム面：亜鉛鉄板焼付／看板:額緑木製／看板面:アクリル
j. のむら工芸

a. CAFÉ RESTAURANT DONKEY PAPA
b. Himeji-shi, Hyogo
c. Café Restaurant Donkey Papa
d. Kunihiro Nomura
e. Kunihiro Nomura
f. Nomura Kougei
g. Yukihiro Imamura
i. Frame surface : Baking paint on galvanized steel plate ; Sign board casing : Acryl
j. Nomura Kougei

a. 軽井沢サムタイムハウス
b. 長野県北佐久郡軽井沢町
c. 日本たばこ産業
d. 匹田定嘉（電通映画社）
e. 設計企画=塚原正一／キャラクター=高橋新三／川崎修司／照明=海藤春樹
f. 小林工芸社
g. 高橋克明
h. 風と太陽をいっぱい取り入れるべくオープンな形にこだわり，建物自体をサインとした.
i. 鉄骨軸組／角材／合板ベニヤ／塗装仕上
j. 小林工芸社

a. KARUIZAWA SOMETIME HOUSE
b. Karuizawa-machi, Nagano
c. Japan Tobacco Inc.
d. Sadayoshi Hikita
e. Planning : Syoichi Tsukahara / Character : Shinzo Takahashi, Syuji Kawasaki / Lighting : Haruki Kaito
f. Kobayashi Kogeisha Co., Ltd.
g. Katsuaki Takahashi
h. Adhering to an open type configuration to fully introduce wind and the sun, the scheme attempted to form the building itself into the figure of the sign.
i. Steel frame work / Square bar / Polycarbonate wood / Painting finish
j. Kobayashi Kogeisha Co., Ltd.

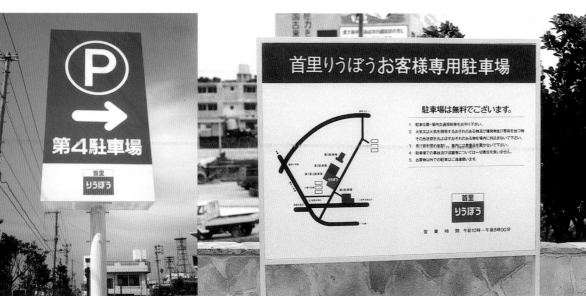

a. 駐車場サイン
b. 沖縄県那覇市
c. 西友
d. 飯田修市
e. 宇野良子
f. 小林工芸社
g. 飯田修市
i. 鋼板／カッティングシート
j. 小林工芸社

a. PARKING SIGN
b. Naha-shi, Okinawa
c. Seiyu Co., Ltd.
d. Shuichi Iida
e. Yoshiko Uno
f. Kobayashi Kogeisha Co., Ltd.
g. Shuichi Iida
i. Steel plate / Cutting sheet
j. Kobayashi Kogeisha Co., Ltd.

●ディレクター，イラストレーター，エージェンシー，エンジニア，音楽，監理者，企画構成，キャラクター，グラフィックデザイナー，コーディネーター，照明，設計，設計監修，設計協力，造形デザイナー，彫刻，テクニカルデザイナー，展示設計，デザイナー，デザイン計画，人形デザイン，背景画，プランナー，プロジェクトマネージャー，プロダクトマネージャー，プロモーター，マネージャー，モニュメント etc.

㈱アーク造園設計事務所	☎03・359・5049	〒160	東京都新宿区若葉1・21　マンション離宮53号
㈱アーバンガウス研究所	☎06・448・8580	〒550	大阪府大阪市西区京町堀1・8・31　安田ビル301
アスカデザイン室	☎0256・35・7350	〒955	新潟県三条市一ノ門2・12・34
㈱アラップインターナショナル	☎03・423・3711	〒107	東京都港区南青山2・12・15　南青山2丁目ビル
㈱アルス HED 事業部	☎03・815・2561	〒112	東京都文京区小石川2・21・5
㈱アルス大阪店	☎06・531・9222	〒550	大阪府大阪市西区立売堀1・9・36
㈱石本建築事務所	☎03・262・7161	〒102	東京都千代田区九段南4・6・12
出江寛建築事務所	☎06・364・7875	〒530	大阪府大阪市北区南森町1・2・22
㈱イセキ	☎03・352・1881	〒151	東京都渋谷区千駄ヶ谷5・30・11
㈱ AUR 建築・都市・研究コンサルタント	☎03・456・2731	〒106	東京都港区麻布十番2・3・5　日勝亭ビル
㈱ L.A.U. 都市施設研究所	☎03・353・0715	〒160	東京都新宿区舟町8・4　北原ビル1F
㈱エンジニアリングフジ	☎03・404・5441	〒107	東京都港区南青山3・11・10
㈱大林組東京本社一級建築士事務所	☎03・296・5880	〒101	東京都千代田区神田錦町3・20
㈱大林組東京本社設計第二部	☎03・296・5879	〒101	東京都千代田区神田錦町3・20
㈱大林組本店設計第二部	☎06・946・4704	〒540	大阪府大阪市東区京橋3・37
鹿島建設㈱建築設計本部	☎03・344・2111	〒163	東京都新宿区西新宿2・1・1　新宿三井ビル29F
㈱環境設計研究室　川瀬篤美	☎03・502・6248	〒105	東京都港区虎ノ門2・8・10　第15森ビル
㈱グッドスピンアーキテクト	☎03・770・5851	〒150	東京都渋谷区猿楽町9・8　代官山パークサイドビレッジ203
㈱景観設計研究所	☎06・354・0407	〒530	大阪府大阪市北区天神橋2・5・2・28　千代田第2ビル10F
㈱公園緑地設計事務所	☎0262・44・1420	〒380	長野県長野市吉田5・22・22　柴崎第2ビル3F
㈱小島ディレクターズ	☎06・445・0373	〒550	大阪府大阪市西区江戸堀1・18
㈱小林工芸社	☎03・940・3022	〒170	東京都豊島区北大塚1・9・15
㈱サエグサ・都市・建築設計事務所	☎0488・85・7323	〒336	埼玉県浦和市大東3・27・9　兼杉ビル3F
佐々木著建築設計室	☎082・249・7633	〒730	広島県広島市中区住吉町15・3・802
㈱ GK グラフィックス	☎03・971・8121	〒171	東京都豊島区南池袋1・11・22　山種ビル7F
㈱ GK 設計	☎03・989・9511	〒171	東京都豊島区南池袋1・11・22　山種ビル6F
㈱ジャパンアートプランニングセンター	☎03・496・0218	〒150	東京都渋谷区神南1・4・2　神南ハイム305
スイス設計㈱	☎011・251・1320	〒060	北海道札幌市中央区南三条3丁目　竹内ビル9F
スペースデザイン・ハッピー	☎03・674・1327	〒124	東京都葛飾区新小岩1・37・5
清家省二	☎03・353・0715	〒160	東京都新宿区舟町8・4　北原ビル1F　㈱L.A.U.都市施設研究所
関俊郎	☎03・455・1171	〒108	東京都港区芝浦4・6・4　㈱乃村工藝社
㈱千伝社	☎06・372・2471	〒531	大阪府大阪市大淀区豊崎6・6・15
㈱船場	☎03・255・7244	〒101	東京都千代田区神田須田町2・1
㈱船場 SC 綜合開発研究所	☎06・313・1008	〒530	大阪府大阪市北区堂山町1・5　大阪合同ビル
SEMBA 設計事務所札幌	☎011・281・1008	〒060	北海道札幌市中央区北五条西13丁目

㈲綜合デザインセンター	☎052・763・4831	〒464	愛知県名古屋市千種区高見1・26・4　タカミ光ビル201
㈱創造社	☎03・353・2211	〒162	東京都新宿区住吉町8・17
大成建設㈱設計本部	☎03・348・1111	〒163	東京都新宿区西新宿1・25・1　新宿センタービル
㈱竹中工務店	☎06・252・1201	〒541	大阪府大阪市東区本町4・27
大昌工芸㈱	☎082・291・6211	〒733	広島県広島市西区小河内町2・15・2
㈱テイ・グラバー	☎03・779・6121	〒141	東京都品川区西五反田3・7・14　興和三信ビル9F
デンコー㈱	☎03・543・1234	〒104	東京都中央区銀座3・15・8
㈱東畑建築事務所東京事務所	☎03・581・1251	〒100	東京都千代田区永田町2・4・3　永田町ビル3F
野老設計事務所	☎03・359・9571	〒160	東京都新宿区四谷3・14　針萬西ビル410
戸田建設㈱	☎03・562・6111	〒104	東京都中央区京橋1・7・1　新八重洲ビル
中島幹夫	☎0474・75・5097	〒274	千葉県船橋市前原東2・13・14
㈱中村建築設計事務所	☎075・492・5201	〒603	京都府京都市北区大宮南椿原町8・5
西山正幸昴工房	☎0286・62・3969	〒321	栃木県宇都宮市平出工業団地44・14
日本街路灯製造㈱	☎052・681・2181	〒456	愛知県名古屋市熱田区五本松町1・8
ニッテン設計事務所㈱ニッテン	☎03・263・7704	〒102	東京都千代田区平河町1・8・13　和田ビル4F
㈱ノミック	☎06・583・3113	〒552	大阪府大阪市港区市岡元町1・1・24　豊島ビル2F
㈱乃村工藝社	☎03・455・1171	〒108	東京都港区芝浦4・6・4
㈱乃村工藝社	☎06・633・3331	〒556	大阪府大阪市浪速区元町1・2・6
㈱乃村工藝社　商業施設開発事業部	☎06・633・3331	〒556	大阪府大阪市浪速区元町1・2・6
㈲のむら工芸	☎0792・36・1621	〒672	兵庫県姫路市飾磨区若宮町25・1
萩原克彦設計事務所	☎03・427・7752	〒154	東京都世田谷区駒沢2・52・3
㈱長谷川工務店	☎03・456・6011	〒105	東京都港区芝2・32・1
企業組合　針谷建築事務所	☎0542・81・1155	〒422	静岡県静岡市小黒3・6・9
ピクデザイン事務所	☎06・358・5265	〒534	大阪府大阪市都島区中野町4・7・12
㈱富士建築設計事務所	☎06・252・7741	〒541	大阪府大阪市東区横堀5・13
㈱ベル環境計画事務所	☎0425・25・4560	〒190	東京都立川市柴崎町2・2・4　ライジングサンビル4F
本間利雄設計事務所＋地域環境計画研究所	☎0236・41・7711	〒990	山形県山形市小白川町413・12
㈱松田平田坂本設計事務所横浜支所	☎045・314・2001	〒220	神奈川県横浜市西区北幸1・11・5　相鉄 KS ビル
三井建設㈱設計部建築第二設計室	☎03・864・3787	〒101	東京都千代田区岩本町3・10・1
三井建設㈱横浜支店	☎045・664・5720	〒231	神奈川県横浜市中区尾上町4・58・60
三菱地所㈱	☎03・287・5811	〒100	東京都千代田区丸の内2・4・1
㈱ヤシマ	☎03・784・2211	〒142	東京都品川区荏原2・3・18
横沢英一	☎0423・66・1167	〒183	東京都府中市本宿町1・32・1　サンライズビル7・203
㈱ヨコタデザインワークスタジオ	☎03・464・6087	〒150	東京都渋谷区猿楽町9・8　代官山パークサイドビレッジ303
㈱渡辺建築事務所	☎03・987・1946	〒171	東京都豊島区雑司が谷3・4・1

環境デザインベストセレクション 2
Environmental Design
Best Selection 2

発行　1987年10月25日初版第1刷発行

編集　グラフィック社編集部
監修　オレンジブック編集部＋寺澤　勉
装丁　株式会社高間デザイン室
本文レイアウト　㈱田村祐介デザイン事務所
カバー写真提供　K.K.川澄建築写真事務所　他

発行者　久世利郎
印刷・製本　錦明印刷株式会社
写植　三和写真工芸株式会社
用紙　三陽国策パルプ株式会社
発行所　株式会社グラフィック社
　　　　〒102 東京都千代田区九段北1-9-12
　　　　Tel. 03-263-4318　振替・東京3-114345

定価　12,500円

ISBN4-7661-0444-7　C3070　¥12500E